REVIVAL BY THE RIVER

THE RESURGENCE OF THE PITTSBURGH PIRATES

Pittsburgh Post-Gazette®

Marlon Byrd (right) celebrates with teammates Jose Tabata (left) and Clint Barmes after Byrd homered in his first game as a Pirate on August 28.

This book is available in quantity at special discounts for your group or organization. For further information contact:

Triumph Books
814 North Franklin Street
Chicago, IL 60610
Phone: (312) 337-0747
www.triumphbooks.com

Printed in the U.S.A.
ISBN: 978-1-60078-968-7

Pittsburgh Post-Gazette
John Robinson Block, Co-publisher and Editor-in-Chief
David M. Shribman, Executive Editor and Vice-President
Susan L. Smith, Managing Editor
Mark J. Rochester, Deputy Managing Editor
Jerry Micco, Assistant Managing Editor, Sports

BOOK EDITOR
Donna Eyring, Sports Editor

PHOTO EDITOR
Andy Starnes

PHOTOGRAPHERS
Peter Diana
Bob Donaldson
Matt Freed
John Heller
Marlene Karas, Pittsburgh Press

ADMINISTRATIVE COORDINATOR
Allison Latcheran, Marketing Manager

Content packaged by Mojo Media, Inc.
Joe Funk: Editor
Jason Hinman: Creative Director

CONTENTS

INTRODUCTION

By David M. Shribman

How we love the rituals of summer: The sweet peaches and juicy melons. The long cool light of evening. The guilty-pleasure novels we wouldn't touch in winter. The rainbow following an afternoon shower. The pennant run of a ballclub picked to go nowhere, determined to go where no expert thought it might.

We had a wonderful summer here in Pittsburgh, a honeydew-and-rainbow kind of summer, a dreamy season of high spirits and high hopes. Our local ballteam, for two decades a patchwork of has-beens (superannuated refugees from somewhere else) and will-bes (angular young men poised for greatness, always somewhere else) was on one of those highs that make for summer reveries, for, finally, this was the year — the year the Pirates broke a two-decade long string of infamy and obloquy, the year we didn't end with somber meditations on the vanity of human wishes and the futility of men left on base.

We had these high hopes last year, and the year before, too. Our Bucs — that's short for buccaneers, a word whose derivation, from French, has something to do with smoked meat, which is how the team finished the season both those years — didn't let us down.

Sure, there were bumps in the road: leads wasted, rallies thwarted, balls dropped in left field. One night, a steamy one at our lovely ballyard on the Allegheny, Jeff Locke pitched a beaut of a game but had no offensive support. A nice performance, surrendering only 3 hits in 7 innings — wasted. That happened. These things do.

But this was not a team destined to be remembered, with the 1951 Brooklyn Dodgers and the 1964 Philadelphia Phillies, as an example of a really good team that collapsed on the path to glory. These Pirates were not the baseball equivalents of President Samuel J. Tilden. (Look him up. He's not on your presidential ruler.)

This was more a team of destiny than a team destined to disappoint. One of the many delights of this team was Locke, barely named to the starting rotation in April only to be named to the All-Star Game in July. You may know that he's from the tiny village of Redstone, N.H., and that New Hampshire's own Alan B. Shepard Jr. rode a Redstone booster into space in 1961, but it was the great Lloyd Jones, chronicler of the White Mountains sports scene, who had the wit to dub him the Redstone Rocket. Take that, Roger Clemens.

But Locke wasn't the only one, or the main one. This was a pitching staff to remember, with a battery mate (Russell

Andrew McCutchen (left) celebrates with Travis Snider after Snider hit the game-winning RBI single in the 11th inning of the Pirates' June 2 win over the Cincinnati Reds.

Martin) who had the season of his career while having the time of his life. The stars glittered at third and at second. There was stardust over the remarkable figure in center field, and in left the one muffed ball only served to underline what a future there is for Starling Marte.

Earlier promising Pirates teams did have a whiff of the buccaneer to them, all swashbuckle but, alas, no belt. This season's team seemed to sail more of a sloop than a Pirate ship, with a couple of head sails (Andrew McCutchen and Francisco Liriano) forward of the mast. Not that there was always smooth sailing ahead. Pirates fans knew those waters.

Indeed, the curious thing is that, as Sen. Edward M. Kennedy, himself something of an ancient mariner, once said in an entirely different context, the hope still lived and the dream didn't die at PNC Park this summer.

Even amid a worrisome losing streak, there was a special grace to these Bucs, a lyricism in how, on every night but one, Marte pulled down a long fly in left, right there at the warning path, and then flipped the ball to a child in the bleachers in one long legato motion; or in how McCutchen exceeded expectations not only at the plate during the game but also along the third base side beforehand, lingering longer than any All Star, signing all manner of baseballs, programs and uniform shirts.

These men were the boys of a generation's summer, at long last.

Because every generation of sports fans, in every city, but especially for this generation of fans in Pittsburgh, deserved a summer seared in memory — a summer romance with the crackle of a play-by-play announcer as our song, unforgettable as a first kiss, as tingly in memory as in the moment, maybe more.

And all the more beautiful the more unexpected it was.

That's why all of the baseball faithful, except maybe for Reds and Cardinals fans, were Pirates partisans once the game resumed after its annual July intermission. It wasn't only because the Pirates had the longest string of losing seasons in the history of American big-time pro sports. It was also because it's almost as stirring to watch a love story as to live one.

We lived it, truly we did, a "Casablanca" by the river bank, and what all of you beyond the Allegheny Mountains were watching was the quiet transformation of the sporting culture of an entire region.

Since the 1974 draft, which produced four NFL Hall of Famers, the Steelers have ruled here. The Penguins, despite their June 2013 collapse, are a team possessed of great ingenuity on the ice and great insights in the front office.

That left the Pirates as the forgotten men of the three rivers, resented for bungling season after season, reviled by true fans for despoiling their jewel of a ballpark with senseless between-innings distractions that seemed designed to be so mindless that the performances on the field might seem artful by comparison.

But this year — this splendid season — people fell in love in Pittsburgh again, with baseball — a game of surpassing beauty, with its own rhythms and its mysterious inner integrity. They fell in love with these Pirates, and also with the idea of being in love. Together we said: Bring it on, with hearts and flowers, and a Whitman's sampler of chocolates, and moonlight and love songs, never out of date. It was an as-time-goes-by kind of moment here in Pittsburgh — you could sense it in the streets and in the stands — for it was still the same old story, a fight for love and glory, a case of do or die. The difference this time is that they didn't die, and that we had a season to remember — a season to cherish — all our lives.

David M. Shribman
Executive Editor
Pittsburgh Post-Gazette

Clouds loom over PNC Park before the Pirates' July 10 game against the Oakland Athletics. The first pitch was delayed more than three hours.

At Commonwealth Press on Pittsburgh's Carson Street, this sign in the front window counted down the wins needed for the Pirates to clinch a winning season. Here Marissa Mack changes numbers after the Pirates topped the Milwaukee Brewers on September 3 for Pittsburgh's 81st win of the season.

WINS

RSE IS LIFTED

WINNERS AT LAST

RAISING THE JOLLY ROGER

2013 Pirates Validate Pride of Fans Who Never Accepted Losing

By Gene Collier

Until now you could only raise it, but now you can praise it as well, because the tattered and battered Jolly Roger now flies over a winning franchise and an ever-resilient city where baseball pride is again validated at long last.

That any franchise in any major sport could erect the kind of futility infrastructure that spanned two full decades of uninterrupted failure was almost incomprehensible, but there was nothing in any way unpredictable about this town's reaction to all that losing.

Pittsburgh hated it.

The Pirates, such as they've been for the 20 consecutive summers leading to this one, were never considered lovable losers around here, were never given even a temporary license to stink with impunity like the long-suffering Chicago Cubs and their insufferable "We Wubs Da Cubs," audience or the 120-loss New York Mets of 1962, who were at least comical.

Not here, buddy.

This town finds losing about as cuddly as a wharf rat.

What various ownership groups pushed onto the field here beginning in 1993 was never considered anything but tremendously annoying, completely embarrassing and shamefully unworthy of a baseball stage erected by Honus Wagner and the Waners, a baseball stage polished to an ornate majesty by Clemente and Stargell, a baseball stage that once delivered performances that solidified Pittsburgh's station in baseball's pantheon.

Even after an uninterrupted two-decade nosedive unmatched in sports history, the Pirates were winners still in the city where they won nine pennants and five World Series and produced 40 Hall of Famers.

Then, somehow, they produced something else: a lost generation of fans who never felt any kind of Pirates pride, at least not authentically, not first hand. Those poor kids. Even when a sort-of pennant race got whipped up by the 1997 "Freak Show" Pirates, working within the seriously terrible National League Central on a total team payroll of $9 million, they finished second with a record of 79-83, five games behind the wholly forgettable Houston Astros.

How they did all that isn't the kind of thing that can be explained in a sports column. That takes a novella at the minimum, perhaps a doctoral thesis or a feature length slasher film, but regardless of the platform, it starts with the coin of the realm: talent.

The Pirates didn't wade into this; they threw themselves off a cliff. There were winners of three consecutive division titles and were standing a single out from the 1992 World Series when they decided they couldn't or wouldn't or shouldn't compete financially with the clubs who would be sweet-talking their talented free agents.

Andrew McCutchen gives the Zoltan sign after doubling against the Cardinals in St. Louis on September 7. The Pirates adopted the Zoltan sign — taken from the movie *Dude, Where's My Car* — during the 2012 season. Players give the sign to teammates after each Pirates extra-base hit.

So once upon a time you watched a prodigy, a wisp of a left-fielder named Barry Bonds, playing left and crushing baseballs, and suddenly you were staring at Orlando Merced, then Orlando Merced and Dave Clark, then Dave Clark and Will Pennyfeather, then Jermaine Allensworth and Keith Osik and Mike Benjamin and Brant Brown, then Kris Benson and Jimmy Anderson and Pat Meares and John Vander Wal, then Tike Redman and Adam Hyzdu, and there goes Ramon Martinez running straight from the PNC Park mound into retirement without so much as a change of clothes, then you were looking at Raul Mondesi disappearing into thin air on a bereavement mission, then it was Jose Castillo and wiener wacking Randall Simon and Ian Snell, and then, the 2009 Pittsburgh Pirates were led by RBI machine Andy LaRoche.

Not Adam LaRoche, Andy LaRoche.

He drove in 64.

A year later, the so-called first season of the new Pirates dynasty ended with a record of 57-105.

But for every combination of player personnel management threw the dice on for two decades, the larger issue was that the dice weren't as faulty as the shooters. Pittsburgh earned its tawdry loser stripes from the top down, failing spectacularly at drafting, scouting, player development, hiring, firing, public relations, etc.

They failed spectacularly at just about everything but ballpark building, providing the oft-acknowledged best ballpark in baseball as the breath-taking theater for a brand of baseball that was consistently bad except for those times when it was all but irredeemably bad.

The 2013 Pirates never acknowledged a winning season as their primary mission. They never accepted 20 consecutive losing seasons as primarily their burden. But Neil Walker lived it, and plenty of others have heard way too much of this history lesson.

That they eventually changed the course of franchise history isn't something that will soon be forgotten. They didn't just raise the Jolly Roger. They honor

Pirates players warm up on the field at Busch Stadium in St. Louis before taking on the Cardinals on September 8. St. Louis and Pittsburgh battled for the National League Central lead throughout the 2013 season.

LOSERS NO MORE

Pirates' Win Ends Two Decades of Futility

By Bill Brink · September 4, 2013

With one word, Andrew McCutchen summarized the feelings of his organization and dismissed two decades of woeful Pirates history. "Nope."

The question wasn't even complete yet and already he knew the answer. Nope, Mr. McCutchen doesn't care that the Pirates' next win will be their 82nd of 2013, securing a winning season for the first time since 1992. They moved one step closer to that long-elusive goal with victory No. 81 — assured of a record of at least .500 for the first time in two decades — defeating the Milwaukee Brewers, 4-3, at Miller Park.

In a surprising season in which they are jostling with the St. Louis Cardinals for first place in their division and had the best record in Major League baseball at the end of July, they are losers no more, but not quite yet winners.

Most — but not all — players and members of the organization no longer care about compiling a winning season. Some say they're past that. Some say it distracts from the immediate task at hand. Some say mediocrity is not the goal.

"I think that if we were any other organization, you probably wouldn't [care] and the question probably wouldn't even be asked," Neil Walker said. "The fact that 82 wins is such a big number in this city because of obvious reasons, it holds a lot more weight."

Mr. McCutchen made his major league debut June 4, 2009, giving him the most playing time on the active roster of anyone in the organization. (Jeff Karstens made his Pirates debut in 2008, but has not pitched this season due to injury.) Mr. McCutchen said fretting about winning 82 games, or a playoff berth for that matter, distracts from the most important focal point: winning that night's game.

"You're putting pressure on yourself when you do that," he said. "Thinking about playoffs, wild cards, teams winning and losing. You're putting added pressure on yourself that you don't need to put on yourself. You can't control what other teams do."

Mr. Walker debuted not long after Mr. McCutchen (Sept. 1, 2009). Mr. Walker, you might have heard, is from around these parts, so he understands the significance of the losing streak outside the prism of this current team.

"If you're asking me, as a fan, as a growing-up fan … that number has some significance, yes," he said. "To the other 24 guys, I don't think it holds that much weight."

In 1992, the Pirates won 96 games, finished first in the National League East and lost to the Atlanta Braves in the National League Championship Series. Since that time, they have not won more than 79 games in a season until now. Their 82nd win in a 162-game season would ensure that even if they lost every single game the rest of the way, they would finish with a .506 winning percentage and end the streak. That's not enough for the current crew.

"The ring is the goal," said hitting coach Jay Bell, a shortstop on the 1992 Pirates and owner of a World Series ring. "That's the prize. As you go through the course of a

Travis Snider celebrates as he crosses home plate following Snider's pinch-hit home run in the ninth inning in Milwaukee, which clinched the Pirates' 81st win of the 2013 season. (AP Images)

season, that's what you're looking to obtain all year long. Getting over .500 is not the goal by any means."

That streak, by the way, remains the longest in the history of North American professional sports. The Philadelphia Phillies held the previous Major League Baseball record with 16 consecutive losing seasons from 1933-48.

The NHL's Vancouver Canucks (1976-91) and the NBA's Kansas City/Sacramento Kings (1983-98) each lost for 15 consecutive years. The NFL's Tampa Bay Buccaneers finished below .500 for 14 consecutive seasons (1983-96).

Despite the implications, few members of the organization perceive ending the streak as a worthy achievement.

"Never been a goal," Pirates president Frank Coonelly said. "Not counting down the days for that, counting the days that we can hoist the National League Central flag at PNC Park."

The previous time the Pirates had a winning season, Mr. Coonelly was practicing law in Washington, D.C., and advising Major League Baseball during negotiations that eventually resulted in the strike-shortened 1994 season. He joined the Pirates in 2007 and witnesses the transformation daily, especially among the fans.

"This year they're in their seats earlier, they're locked in for the first pitch, so they're getting to the ballpark earlier because they see something special happening," he said.

Mr. Coonelly spoke recently in the visitors dugout at Petco Park in San Diego. Behind him, some of the Pirates displayed no sense of urgency. Instead they laughed at a reenactment of first-base coach Rick Sofield's tumble down the steps the previous night and a chalk outline of his body on the dugout floor.

Few people spend as much time around the team as clubhouse manager Scott Bonnett. "Bones" to players and colleagues, he was a 20-year-old batboy in Cincinnati when the Reds won the 1990 World Series. He joined the Pirates before the 2000 season, so he has seen his share of winning and losing clubhouses.

"In years past, you heard … they're keeping track of how many games over [.500]," Mr. Bonnett said. "This year, you haven't heard it."

Mr. Bonnett credited manager Clint Hurdle's positive demeanor and the addition of catcher Russell Martin with improving the on-field product and the cohesion of the clubhouse, which in a sport such as baseball, with such a large individual component, is not always necessary for a successful team.

"This year they've been there, done that, and somehow they all are rooting for each other and you don't see that often," Mr. Bonnett said. "Everybody's hanging out with everybody, everybody's having fun with each other."

His view of breaking the streak echoed others in the franchise: "A couple years ago .500 meant a lot. Now, I don't want .500. I want pennants. Championships."

An 82nd win remains important in the sense that they have to win an 82nd game before they can win, say, a 94th game, and the last thing the Pirates want to do is see a one-game wild-card loss wash away their greatest season since Barry Bonds and Doug Drabek. They want the division.

"That's 162 days of hard work and then you go play one game, and if you don't play good that day then you head to the house," Mr. Hurdle said. "That's going to be a hard pill to swallow every year for a couple teams."

He often reminds people that his current team has not lost for 20 seasons. He's in year three. Mr. Coonelly is in year six, Mr. McCutchen and Mr. Walker in year five, Mr. Bell in year one. "Our vision will be to win the division," he said. "It won't be to win more games than we lose."

As pervasive as the lack of thought given to 82 is, it is not all-encompassing. Charlie Morton joined the Pirates in the trade that cleared a spot for the team to call up Mr. McCutchen. Mr. Morton made his Pirates debut six days after Mr. McCutchen did. Mr. Morton cares.

"It's been 20 years of losing," he said. "It does matter to put a winning team out there for a lot of people and for the city. That's not our goal but it's the byproduct of having a good team.

"Say [the Pirates] never went to the playoffs, but won 82 games every year. There wouldn't be that shadow kind of following the city around. I describe it as kind of like a relief." ∎

Andrew McCutchen singles during the third inning of the Pirates' win over the Milwaukee Brewers on September 3. After the game, McCutchen insisted that Pirates players were not focused on ending the franchise's streak of 20 straight losing seasons. "You're putting pressure on yourself when you do that," he said. (AP Images)

81ST WIN ENDS RUN OF LOSING SEASONS

Pirates Ride Snider's Homer to Beat Brewers, 4-3

By Bill Brink · September 3, 2013

Now the Pirates find themselves in a sort of limbo.

After their 4-3 win against the Milwaukee Brewers at Miller Park, they have 81 victories this season. It is unlikely the Pirates will lose all their 24 remaining games, but, if they do, they have ensured a finish of at least .500 for the first time since 1992.

"It's just a win, man," said Travis Snider, whose pinch-hit home run in the ninth inning put the Pirates ahead. "We got a lot more baseball to play. Getting caught up in that personal achievements is not what we're here for."

Most of the players don't care about that. More important for the current team, the win moved the Pirates two games ahead of the St. Louis Cardinals in the NL Central. The Cardinals lost to the Cincinnati Reds for the second night in a row, this time by 1-0.

"We're just playing to win a World Series," said Andrew McCutchen, who also homered. "That's what we're here for. That's what it's all about. We're one step closer every day."

Nothing changed in the clubhouse. Players ate spaghetti and meatballs in silence — the music usually playing after wins was turned down so the media could interview Snider — and watched highlights from around the league. Manager Clint Hurdle patiently answered questions about the losing streak, as he has all year.

"It's a step in the right direction," he said. "It was on our to-do list."

Snider homered off Jim Henderson to break a 3-3 tie. It was his fourth home run this season and first since June 15.

He came off the disabled list Sunday after missing August due to pain in his left big toe.

"Going down to Triple-A, Double-A, getting the at-bats, playing on a regular basis, addressing some of the mechanical breakdowns that have been caused over the last couple months — things weren't right," Snider said. "I felt like I had a good run down there and felt confident coming up here whatever role they were going to put me in to just go out there and compete."

McCutchen hit his 18th homer this season and 100th of his career, in the first. He clobbered Yovani Gallardo's 2-2 fastball to left-center.

"It's definitely a great milestone for myself to be able to do that," McCutchen said.

McCutchen noted that the Pirates don't play to break even, but allowed that the season has been enjoyable.

"It's one of those things, it feels like a dream almost because we've had a lot of years of losing and now that we're winning and we're continuing to get better, it's fun to be a part of," he said.

The new additions pitched in Tuesday.

Marlon Byrd went 2 for 3 with two RBIs and Justin Morneau went 3 for 3.

"It's nice being a part of this," Byrd said. "I'm just a piece of the puzzle, come in, drive in runs whenever I can and help the team win."

Byrd has been a Pirate for seven games, but already adopted the clubhouse's approach to dealing with the losing streak.

"We have one focus," he said, "and that's getting to the playoffs and winning the whole thing."

Travis Snider launches a solo home run off of Milwaukee's Jim Henderson in the top of the ninth inning to break a 3-3 tie. The win was the Pirates' 81st of the 2013 season, ending the Pirates' streak of 20 straight seasons with a losing record.

The game proceeded into the eighth tied at 2-2 before Byrd gave the Pirates the lead. McCutchen walked and took third on Morneau's single. Byrd doubled down the left-field line to score McCutchen.

The Brewers tied it in the bottom half of the eighth, though. Vin Mazzaro issued a leadoff walk to Caleb Gindl, who took second on Norichika Aoki's grounder. Jean Segura singled home Gindl to tie the score, 3-3.

Earlier this season, Hurdle talked to the Clemente family — relatives of Roberto Clemente, the iconic Pirate who wore No. 21.

"They told me that we can't have 21 losing seasons," Hurdle said. "We've got to find a way to not have Roberto's number tied to that. I told them we would do anything we could to take care of that, and that's been taken care of."

Francisco Liriano takes the mound tonight when the Pirates try for their 82nd win, which all but guarantees their first winning season since 1992. There's basically no chance the Pirates and a few other teams suffer losing streaks that result in a one-game playoff and an 81-82 record. Barring that, they hover, not yet assured winners but no longer losers, either. ■

20 YEARS OF FUTILITY

Atlanta's Sid Bream slides past the tag of Pittsburgh catcher Mike LaValliere to score the winning run in Game 7 of the 1992 National League Championship Series. Prior to 2013, 1992 marked the last season the Pirates finished with a winning record. (Getty Images)

THE PLAY THAT STARTED THE SLIDE

Pirates' Legacy of Losing Began with Sid Bream

By J. Brady McCollough · April 1, 2012

The Pirates of 1992 are not the type to believe in the supernatural. They are tried-and-true baseball men, believing only that, when round ball hits round bat, anything can happen.

Still, they look for answers — ways to explain the events of an autumn night in Atlanta that now feels predestined.

"All the stars lined up against us," said Andy Van Slyke, then the Pirates center fielder.

To wonder if the cosmos were working extra hard on Oct. 14, 1992, is understandable. Thursday's opening day at PNC Park will begin the 20th season since the Pirates lost to the Braves, 3-2, in Game 7 of the National League Championship Series, and Pittsburgh is still waiting for a winning baseball team to return. Two decades of losing is inexplicable, but to say it's a curse? No, the Pirates of 1992 won't go down that road.

But they'll live each day with the pain, a loyal companion all these years. Numerous times, Van Slyke has replayed the bottom of the ninth and argued strikes that were called balls. Mike LaValliere, then the Pirates catcher, has never watched again. Can't. Won't.

"It's just a terrible memory," he said. "It's just kind of a wound that's there that I'd be picking at. Just let it stay where it is."

Jose Lind, then the Pirates second baseman, can't bring himself to tune into postseason baseball at all. His error on a David Justice ground ball simply won't go away.

"It still haunts me now," Lind said. "If I catch that ball, we probably go to the World Series."

Lind had made six errors that entire season. If he hadn't made that one, maybe Sid Bream never would have ended up on second base as the potential game-winning run.

Bream's slide under the sweeping tag of LaValliere created what is now known by some fans as the "Bream Curse," and, to see how the other side of that fateful night lives, you don't have to travel far.

Two decades after his family received death threats and a less-threatening toilet-papering of their Wexford home, Bream resides in Zelienople — at the top of a hill in pure Western Pennsylvania daylight.

Bream, born near Harrisburg in Carlisle, played for the Pirates for five years before being traded to the Braves. He considers this region his home and still cheers for the Pirates, but he can't deny that his life changed at their expense.

On the wall to the right of the large TV in the living room, a painting of his slide and the ensuing celebration hangs proudly.

Bream's fame helped him develop a motivational-speaking career. Before each speech, he shows the clip of that Game 7.

Sid Bream, then the Pirates first baseman, shares an embrace with manager Jim Leyland in 1988. Bream played five seasons for the Pirates before signing with the Atlanta Braves after the 1990 season, but the Carlisle, Pennsylvania, native is best remembered by Pirates fans for scoring the run that ended the Pirates' playoff run in 1992.

Shaine Patsievas of Seneca Valley High School gets some batting pointers from Sid Bream in 2005. Bream remained in the Pittsburgh area after retiring and today lives in Zelienople.

"If it wasn't for this play," Bream tells his audiences, "I doubt very much I'd be standing here in front of you."

He has watched the play hundreds of times, and, with each viewing, he believes one thing more and more: His beating of Barry Bonds' throw from left field — and everything that led up to it — was nothing other than an act of God.

PARTING WAYS

The seeds of 1992 began to sprout two years earlier. After falling to the Cincinnati Reds four games to two in the 1990 NLCS, the Pirates had a decision to make about first baseman Sid Bream, whose contract was up.

He was a solid everyday player, and he had played a part in the Pirates' rise under manager Jim Leyland, but Bream had also just turned 30 and carried a creaky right knee.

Bream wanted to stay in Pittsburgh more than anything. As Leyland molded the Pirates from a 104-loss team in 1985 to a 95-win squad in 1990, Bream had built a home here with his wife and two boys. His teammates were now his close friends, and he had even become hunting buddies with Leyland.

Negotiations, however, did not go well. The Pirates did not offer what Bream and his agent considered fair market value, while the Braves did. But it wasn't that simple. The Braves were coming off a last-place, 65-97 finish, while the Pirates were now clear favorites to make the World Series.

"It was a very, very difficult time for my wife, Michelle, and I," Bream said. "We went to bed that night and literally cried all night thinking that we were leaving Pittsburgh."

Bream took the Braves' offer, and it wasn't long before he would be facing his former team in the 1991 regular season. In one of those games, Bream hit the first grand slam of his career, but he hardly could enjoy it.

"I was a wreck in the dugout," Bream said. "Instead of being jubilant for what just happened, I was sad."

The hurt was only beginning. The Braves were on their way to a miraculous season, winning the National League West and becoming the first team in league history to go from last place to first in one year. They would meet the Pirates in the 1991 NLCS, and, behind masterful starting pitching, win the series, 4-3.

"I sat there and thought to myself, 'Good grief, are they going to have another chance?'" Bream said.

THE LAST SHOT

A year later, when Pirates ace Doug Drabek took the mound for the bottom of the ninth, three outs separated Pittsburgh from the World Series.

It had not been an easy ride. After the 1991 season, they lost slugger Bobby Bonilla in free agency. Because the organization couldn't pony up for Bonilla, it was clear that the Pirates also wouldn't be re-signing Bonds and Drabek when their contracts expired after 1992.

The window was already closing fast when they arrived at spring training. And it was during those normally hopeful six weeks that the sand began slipping rapidly through the hourglass.

One day, the Pirates arrived at the clubhouse to find that pitcher John Smiley, who had won 20 games in 1991, had been traded to the Minnesota Twins for two prospects — pitcher Denny Neagle and outfielder Midre Cummings.

"Everybody was absolutely distraught … mad, throwing things," said Bob Walk, then a Pirates starting pitcher. "This was our last year to take a shot at it, and it at least looked like the organization was throwing in the towel."

Leyland called a meeting and told his players that they were still a great team. Sure enough, seven months later, after a 96-66 season and gritty wins in games five and six of the NLCS, there was Drabek on the mound with the ball in his hand and confidence brimming.

The Pirates led the Braves 2-0 when Terry Pendleton came to the plate. Pendleton roped a long fly ball down the right field line,

and Pirates right fielder Cecil Espy shockingly let the ball drop inside the line for a double. That was the first head-shaking play in an improbable ninth.

Next up: Justice. He lined a ground ball to second base. Lind, known by the nickname "Chico," was a Gold Glove second baseman, but the ball hit the top of his hand instead of the webbing of his mitt and bounded into the outfield.

"I mean Chico never boots a ball," Leyland said, "and, I'm not blamin' him, but he boots a ball."

Next up, Bream. He stared across the mound and saw Drabek, one of his closest friends during his time with the Pirates, staring back. Drabek walked Bream on four pitches.

"Our families were close," Bream said. "His wife and my wife and our kids were together constantly, and whether or not that played into his mind … I don't know. He really didn't get close to the strike zone."

With the bases loaded, Leyland removed Drabek from the game and dropped closer Stan Belinda into a harrowing situation.

Next up, Ron Gant, who nearly ended the game with a grand slam but settled for a long out to left. Pendleton scored on a sacrifice fly, bringing the score to 2-1.

Next up, Damon Berryhill, who worked the count to 3-1. Behind the plate, umpire Randy Marsh leaned in behind LaValliere.

Marsh was supposed to be umpiring first base. But, back in the second inning, home plate umpire John McSherry fell ill. McSherry was a heavy-set man, and he had to take a seat.

"He was pale as a ghost," Marsh said.

Marsh would work the rest of the game behind home plate. He was known as a hitter-friendly umpire, and his reputation would prove to be fair.

Against Berryhill, Belinda delivered what appeared to many to be a strike. Marsh called ball four.

"I like that pitch, Randy," LaValliere recalled grumbling to Marsh. "We've got to have that for a strike."

With the bases now loaded again and one out, a helpless feeling spread.

"It was like seeing a crystal vase fall out of someone's hands, and you're watching it in slow motion," said Lanny Frattare, the Pirates' longtime play-by-play man, "and there's just no way you can stop it."

The Pirates had just as much control over the outcome as the Braves, but it no longer felt that way. After Brian Hunter popped out to shortstop, Braves manager Bobby Cox pinch hit with little-used Francisco Cabrera.

The scoreboard still read 2-1 Pirates. There were two outs. And Sid Bream stood on second base with one thing on his mind: Score.

SILENCE SETS IN

Bream knew that he was the last person the Braves would have chosen to be the potential game-winning run. His knee-surgery tally was up to five, but Cox stuck with him.

Several circumstances were working in his favor. First, Bonds was hugging the left field line, and, despite Van Slyke motioning to him to move closer to center, Bonds stayed put. Second, there were two outs, which meant that Bream wouldn't have to hesitate on contact. Third, Bream was taking some liberties with his lead from second base.

"If Stan Belinda would have just stepped off and thrown back," Bream said, "I would have been a goat."

The scouting report on Cabrera, who had just 10 at-bats all season, was that he was a good fastball hitter. So LaValliere called for two breaking pitches to start. Both were balls. After Cabrera lined a fastball foul, bringing the count to 2-1, LaValliere asked for another fastball. Cabrera reached out and hammered the pitch to left for a base hit.

Bonds sped to his left as Bream pumped like an old locomotive. Justice scored, tying the game at 2, but LaValliere figured, with Bream's lack of speed, that the Pirates could get the game to extra innings. But, Bream kept coming, and still, no ball.

"There's a timing to plays," LaValliere said, "and my internal clock was just going. I'm getting edgy. This should be happening a little bit sooner."

Bonds came up with the ball and had to throw across his body. He fired a one-hopper that landed several feet down the first-base line, creating just enough room — an estimated 4 inches — for Bream's famous slide.

Braves 3, Pirates 2.

As Bream was mobbed at home plate, LaValliere slowly trudged toward the dugout.

"I was too numb to even be [angry]," LaValliere said. "I just remember walking off the field, the ball in my glove, and the ball just fell out."

The Pirates of 1992 don't remember much about the aftermath, only silence — in the clubhouse and on the plane back to Pittsburgh.

Bream didn't talk to his former teammates in the days, months and years after his slide to glory. Because, really, what was there to say?

THINKING OF FANS

Twenty years after their greatest disappointment, the Pirates of 1992 no longer think about themselves.

"More than anything, the frustration was — and this was something you really couldn't share with people — but I knew we weren't gonna keep Bonds," Leyland said, "and obviously what was going to happen after that was a little bit of a depressing time. What really hurt was that it hurt the whole city so much."

The Pirates knew their run was temporarily over — but this long?

Van Slyke now lives in the St. Louis area, and he is still a Pirates fan.

"The hardest thing for me is to see what was there and now what exists," Van Slyke said. "It's just hard for me to accept that it's going to be 20 years."

But the idea of the "Bream Curse" is a non-starter with the former Pirates, and Bream doesn't believe in it either.

He's actively tried to help the Pirates start winning again. In 2008, the Pirates hired him as a hitting coach with their Class A short season affiliate, the State College Spikes, but that lasted only one year because Bream didn't like being away from his family.

He gets the feeling other opportunities have dried up because of The Slide.

Bream has given plenty of speeches in Pittsburgh, though, and often someone from the crowd will yell "You were out!" and laughter will fill the room. Enough years have passed now, and, certainly, it is time again for winning baseball on the North Shore.

"I hope and pray that this year, 2012, will be a great year for the Pittsburgh Pirates," Bream said, "and they'll get back to where they should be — on top." ∎

Barry Bonds high-fives teammates after the Pirates defeated the Atlanta Braves 13-4 in Game 6 of the 1992 NLCS. The win left the Pirates just one win away from the National League pennant. Instead, the Pirates lost Game 7 in heartbreaking fashion, Bonds left to sign with the San Francisco Giants, and the Pirates began a streak of 20 consecutive losing seasons. (AP Images)

WIN OR LOSE, PIRATES A PART OF PITTSBURGH

The Torch Is Passed; Let It Be Full of Hope

By Gene Collier • October 4, 2012

You can search all the usual crime scenes in the seedy psychological world that is sub-mediocrity baseball for one, final, oddly emblematic detail from this misbegotten Pirates season, but you probably are going to wind up looking in the wrong place.

You can note with emphasis, perhaps, that, in their final appearance of 2012, the Pirates struck out another 11 times, lifting their season total to a mind-bending 1,354, which comes to more than eight strikeouts every time they drew the lines on the field.

You can prod Pirates manager Clint Hurdle one last time about how he plans to get professional hitters, uh, batters, from making the same correctable mistakes again and again and again and again, as though they are petrified to do things any other way.

"Great question; one way to get a guy's attention, unfortunately, is with the lineup," Hurdle was saying long before a desultory 83rd loss that neither his club nor the postseason-bound Atlanta Braves seemed to have any interest in. "The results are the results, but what we really have to take into account is the effort that goes into the result. In a situation where you're trying to move a runner, is there effort and focus on moving the runner or is there just a swing early in the count to the pull side of the field?"

Again Wednesday, the manager would question neither his club's sense of urgency nor its attitude while it went about losing 36 of the final 52 games.

That its manager thinks this is a club "headed in the right direction," well, that's a case that can be built and effectively presented only to a sympathetic jury, but the last detail of 2012 isn't going to be found in any of those relevant arguments either.

For the last detail, I'll put 20,615, which was the paid attendance Wednesday, representing the final assemblage of known sympathizers this season. Two sat in the extreme upper reaches of PNC Park as the baseball season evaporated into nothing around here for the 20th consecutive summer. One was a man in a TABATA jersey, the other a boy of no more than 4. In the final inning break of 2012, the man posed the little boy with one of those little wooden bats, a black one, and took his picture — a little boy with a little bat in a little cap and a smile as glorious as the approaching sunset.

That'll be the last detail, OK?

Because no matter what happens around here, the game still gets passed from one generation to the next, which is how the game generates its least empirical but most indispensable by-product: Hope.

The passing of that torch isn't always formal, isn't always smooth.

Pirates fans came to PNC Park on April 16, 2013, to honor Kent Tekulve, a star reliever for the Bucs in the 1970s and '80s. After 20 consecutive losing seasons, the Pirates gave fans more than history to cheer about in 2013.

The transition is rarely accompanied by the commanding voice of James Earl Jones, explaining plaintively in *Field of Dreams*, "The one constant through all the years … has been baseball. America has rolled by like an army of steamrollers. It's been erased like a blackboard, rebuilt, and erased again. But baseball has marked the time. This field, this game, is part of our past. It reminds us of all that once was good, and that could be again."

As I sat with my elder son through the final innings Wednesday, I remembered the early parts of our own generational transition.

This was at Three Rivers Stadium, circa 1990; there was a meeting on the mound. Just as Jim Leyland reached the hill, my then 5-year old son asked me what they were talking about.

"Probably about whether they want to walk this batter," I said.

"You mean, walk him on purpose?" he said.

"Uh-huh."

"Why would they do that?"

"Because," I said as something began to dawn on me, "you can make it easier for the fielders to make outs if there are runners on every base, and a walk would load the bases right now."

"Then why wouldn't they walk him?" he said.

"Well," I said, recognizing that this was my transitional moment, the point at which I would start to explain the game to my son, as my father (and mother and aunts and uncles) had to me, as his father to him, "the next hitter is pretty dangerous, and say he doubles. You'll end up allowing three runs instead of two, so you've got to think about it a little."

"One more question," he said.

"Yes," I said, very nearly getting emotional.

"Do you think more people die with their eyes open or closed."

So, yes, it goes in fits and starts.

But there we were Wednesday, me with my sloppily indifferent scorecard and him with his 20-to-30 Pirates games a year habit, a baseball loyalist who'll be 28 before the next spring training arrives. I've passed baseball to him and his brother, but it's Pirates baseball. The Pirates baseball of Generation Lost.

Does that count?

Depends on the hope factor.

"I could have seen an 80th win today," he said. "There have only been five 80-win seasons in my lifetime, so that's something. I've seen power hitting this year like I've never seen here. I've seen a starting pitcher with 16 or 17 wins.

"They've done almost exactly what I expected; they've just done it in a very weird way — all of the winning, then all of the losing."

That sounded vaguely hopeful.

As ever, that will do. ∎

Pirates fans wait out a rain delay at PNC Park in July 2013. Empty seats at Pirates games became a rare sighting in 2013.

BUILDING A WINNER

Pirates players stand for the national anthem at PNC Park on April 15, 2013. All major league players wore No. 42 that day to honor Jackie Robinson.

HOW TO AVOID ANOTHER PITT-FALL

Is It Possible? What Can—and Will—the Pirates Do to Win Early?

By Bill Brink · April 1, 2013

In light of the way the previous two years ended, the second half of the Pirates' 2013 season will attract attention. That includes their performance, the return of some injured pitchers and whom they might add, either from the minor leagues or at the trade deadline.

Before the Pirates can worry about the second half, though, they have to get out of April.

Yes, the Pirates open the season at PNC Park against the Chicago Cubs, who finished 2012 with a 61-101 record. But for the rest of the month, every team the Pirates play finished at least .500 and either made the playoffs or had a chance at a wild-card spot in the fall of 2012.

"We're going to need to be sharp early," general manager Neal Huntington said.

The Pirates finished 2012 with a 79-83 record, seven more wins than in 2011 but still not enough to prevent the streak of losing seasons to reach 20. They finished fourth in the National League Central Division.

After the Cubs, the Pirates travel to Los Angeles to face the Dodgers. After a trip to Phoenix to face the Arizona Diamondbacks, the Pirates return home to face the Cincinnati Reds, St. Louis Cardinals and Atlanta Braves, all 2012 playoff teams. The Philadelphia Phillies, Cardinals and Milwaukee Brewers round out the month.

"One of my beliefs is that you can lose a season in April," said Jay Bell, the Pirates' first-year hitting coach. "You can't win one in April, but you can definitely lose one in April."

The Pirates dug themselves a hole offensively early a year ago, causing the coaching staff to address the thought process needed to start well. They had a .282 team on-base percentage April, .264 in May, a two-month stretch of historically bad offense.

"This camp is set up so that we can prepare for April 1," Bell said. "A lot of times, getting out of the gate early, well, is a mindset. More than anything else, it's the way you approach it mentally."

Part of that occurred because too often, the bottom third of the order presented a three-up, three-down opportunity to opponents. Clint Barmes hit .149 in April, .189 in May, and Rod Barajas was hitting below .200 until mid-May.

Barmes improved in the second half of the season, and Barajas is gone, replaced by Russell Martin. Martin hit .211 with the New York Yankees in 2012, but also hit 21 home runs and is a career .260 hitter.

"There's every reason in the world to believe that he's going to be a much more productive offensive player this year," Huntington said.

The entire offense, led by Andrew McCutchen, compensated in June and July and helped the Pirates to a 59-44 record at the trade deadline. They acquired pitcher Wandy Rodriguez, who was solid down the stretch. They also got Travis Snider, Gaby Sanchez and Chad Qualls, but none of them performed well in the final two months.

When Pirates owner Bob Nutting visited spring camp in February, he cautioned against trading young assets to

Manager Clint Hurdle greets Pirates players during pregame introductions before the team's 2013 home opener at PNC Park.

acquire major league players capable of immediate contribution. He also expressed the desire to commit most of his resources to the opening-day roster, rather than saving some money for the deadline.

"We need to get to the trading deadline in a strong position," Nutting said.

Huntington said the Pirates will evaluate additions when the time comes. They were not comfortable with the types of deals available for impact players before the previous two trading deadlines.

"We were prepared to do that last year, but the market didn't bear it out," he said. "We were prepared to do that two years ago, but the market didn't bear it out."

The minor league system, Huntington said, could provide the necessary currency to improve the major league team if the front office finds a deal it likes.

"We're working to try to have some bats and some position players so that you're not hamstrung because, oh, we can't trade that guy," he said. "There are certain guys you want to hold onto, and the return would have to be significant to be able to even engage in conversation." ∎

STAY HUMBLE, REMEMBER YOUR FAITH

The Story of Pirates Center Fielder Andrew McCutchen Begins With An Earnest Entreaty

By J. Brady McCollough · March 31, 2013

Four men look at an 18-year-old baseball player, and they see a blessing.

The young man sitting in front of them has been picked by the Pittsburgh Pirates in the first round of the 2005 draft, and his life is already changing, to the tune of a $1.9 million signing bonus. The men are at a Red Lobster in Lakeland, Fla., a half-hour's drive from home in the small town of Fort Meade, to pass along some wisdom.

In a matter of days, Andrew McCutchen's professional career will set sail with the Gulf Coast League Pirates. A team scout has told him that he is special, that he could be Pittsburgh's baseball savior, the next Barry Bonds. It's a lot for a teenager to handle, so his father, Lorenzo McCutchen, asked three trusted men of God to help lay a foundation for him to fall back on when the world gets crazy around him.

They are attempting to speak directly into Andrew's heart, about staying true to himself, about keeping God first, about the pitfalls of the fame that could come his way.

"We were giving him his wings," Lorenzo recalls.

As the conversation moves around the table, Andrew is mostly silent.

He does not show his emotions easily, but the men eventually break through. Pastors Pernell Cornelius of Fort Meade, Dexter Howard of Fayetteville, Ark., and Robert Dowell of Lawton, Okla., have noticed Andrew's deep appreciation for the impromptu rite of passage.

By the end of the dinner, tears will gather in Andrew's eyes, and the men will cry together over their seafood.

★★★★★★★★

McCutchen sits at his locker in the Pirates' clubhouse at McKechnie Field in Bradenton, Fla., getting ready to play another spring training game.

It is March 2013, and the prophecy of eight years ago is true. He is the Pirates' star center fielder, a two-time All-Star who finished third in last year's voting for National League Most Valuable Player. He is the face — and the hair — of the franchise, his long locks having become a symbol of hope for a fan base that has had to take loyalty to new levels over two decades.

He's trying to embrace the role, and some days are better than others. The days when he implored his Twitter followers to vote him onto the cover of the popular baseball video game "MLB The Show 2013" and they actually pulled it off — they were good ones. The days when ESPN joined him in Fort Meade to film a feature story to be broadcast for millions — they were OK, too.

McCutchen, known more frequently today as "Cutch," is becoming a household name for baseball fans across the country, and he has hired a publicist to manage his image

Andrew McCutchen connects on a double during the Pirates' 3-1 win over the Braves on April 20. A three-time All-Star, McCutchen led the National League in hits in 2012.

and public appearances. Time has become more valuable, and so too has the need to have control over his privacy.

When a reporter approaches him at his locker and mentions an upcoming visit to Fort Meade, McCutchen is suddenly uncomfortable.

"Everybody wants to know the life story of Andrew McCutchen," he mumbles.

Moments later, an ad plays on the flat-screen TV mounted on the wall of the clubhouse. It features McCutchen on the cover of a video game, along with a fitting marketing slogan for his existence as a 26-year-old:

So real. It's unreal.

What's real and what's not are judgments McCutchen now has to make on a daily basis. Another reporter wants to go to Fort Meade?

"There's nothing there," he says.

Only answers.

LORENZO'S CHALLENGE

Lorenzo McCutchen is a star running back at Fort Meade High School in 1986, a young man who is popular around town because of his charisma, but none of that matters as he walks with his girlfriend, Petrina Swan, into the home of Pastor Pernell Cornelius.

Petrina is like a daughter to "Pastor C," one of the most active teenagers at Peaceful Believers Church. She plays volleyball, and Cornelius hopes she will earn a college scholarship one day.

Lorenzo and Petrina have some news they'd like to share, and when Petrina says she's pregnant, Cornelius is taken aback.

Cornelius asks if Petrina has told her mother yet. She says no.

"He's going with you," Cornelius recalls saying.

Lorenzo will need to be groomed into a man quickly. When the baby is born, Lorenzo will be just a junior in high school. He'll possibly have a chance to play football in college, but where will that take him, other than away from the child? Many young men are unable to shoulder their responsibility, and there is no way of knowing at this point what Lorenzo is made of.

★ ★ ★ ★ ★ ★ ★ ★

Lorenzo McCutchen has a very important job for his roommate, David Needs. They are freshmen in the fall of 1988 at Carson-Newman College in Jefferson City, Tenn., a running back and quarterback, respectively, who are redshirting during their first year on campus.

The phone rings in their dorm room. It's for Lorenzo. David Needs answers and must keep the caller on the line for as long as it takes Lorenzo to return.

"Where's my daddy?" the 2-year-old boy asks.

The father and son talk most nights. Lorenzo pays the phone bill, scrounging up the money just as he would back home, grabbing weekend shifts picking fruit in the fields on top of his steady work as a cook to buy Andrew diapers.

"You could tell that the separation was tough," Needs recalls.

Lorenzo's father had abandoned him as a child, and he'd promised his mother that he would not do the same to Andrew. But, still, as a burly and powerful fullback, he was willing to chase his NFL dream 700 miles away.

Petrina, who is playing volleyball at Polk County (Fla.) Community College, supports him, believing that he should better himself for Andrew's sake.

Lorenzo returns to the room and happily takes the phone. He'll do anything to connect with his son. Knowing that, Needs isn't too surprised when Lorenzo never plays a down of football for Carson-Newman.

★ ★ ★ ★ ★ ★ ★ ★

As a 5-year-old, Andrew McCutchen doesn't quite comprehend the significance of what's happening at Peaceful Believers Church on Aug. 1, 1992. His parents, Lorenzo and Petrina, are getting married.

If Lorenzo had stayed in Tennessee, he'd be a redshirt junior fullback, possibly closer to one dream, but much further from the other. Lorenzo gave up his pursuit of a football career to be near Andrew, coming home after one year to work in the same phosphate mines that once provided shifts to Lorenzo's mother as she raised him.

Upon his return, Lorenzo didn't show himself to be husband material for Petrina, instead living the party life. Petrina made it clear that she wouldn't marry him unless he became a man of God, and she meant it.

On this Saturday afternoon, as Cornelius opens the doors of his church, he knows how far Lorenzo has come since that sobering meeting at his house. Whether leaving school was a wise choice or not, Lorenzo has shown a commitment to family.

"I was very proud," Cornelius recalls. "He hung in there with her through it all. He really stood up as a man, and he would be really good for Trina."

For the town of about 6,000, the bonding of two of their own is a joyous occasion, and now, the McCutchens can begin their life together. Lorenzo has purchased a trailer home in nearby Bartow,

Andrew McCutchen makes his way to the field during 2013 Opening Day ceremonies at PNC Park. McCutchen, who was first called up to the major leagues in June 2009, made his fourth consecutive Opening Day start in center field for the Pirates.

closer to the mines but still an easy drive to the Fort Meade baseball diamonds.

TOWARD A PIRATE'S LIFE

Lorenzo and his son arrive at Field B of the Fort Meade Dixie Youth facility. Lorenzo may be a football player at heart, but his son loves baseball, and so he teaches him the game the only way he knows how — with a little extra force behind it.

"I used to tell him to swing hard and protect his 'house'!" Lorenzo recalls.

The "house," in this instance, is home plate. And when Andrew McCutchen steps into the batter's box and leans over the white, irregularly shaped pentagon, his orders are to think of it as a representation of something bigger.

"His mother and father and sister was inside the house, so he protected his house!" Lorenzo recalls.

Andrew, built slender, unlike his father, sprays balls all over the field using his natural bat speed. When they run out, they collect the balls in the outfield and start again. This scene plays out day after day, month after month, year after year, Andrew protecting his house with each fierce swing of the bat.

He will become the best young player in Fort Meade, and

some of the townspeople will collect money to help send him to Puerto Rico for Roberto Clemente's baseball camp. Then, Fort Meade High coach Jeff Toffanelli will decide he needs him on the varsity as an eighth-grader. He will lead the county high schools in hitting that year, batting over .500.

★★★★★★★★

As a teenager, Andrew McCutchen is not perfect. There are the usual parent-teen entanglements and boundary pushing, and one battle comes to a head after Andrew begins driving a Dodge Dakota truck.

His parents have told him he is not to listen to any music with curse words.

Lorenzo gets in Andrew's truck, turns on the ignition and hears a hip-hop track laced with bad language. Lorenzo takes the CD out of the player and finds his son.

"You know we don't listen to this type of music," Lorenzo says. "That isn't tolerated around here."

Andrew says that the CD is not his, but that doesn't stop Lorenzo from breaking it in half.

★★★★★★★★

The Pirates want to see Andrew in a pressure situation, so they invite the high school senior and potential draft pick to come to Pirate City in Bradenton to take batting practice.

There are questions about whether he can shine on the big stage. He is going to alternate in the cage with Rajai Davis, who plays for Class AA Altoona, to give the Pirates a direct comparison.

Rob Sidwell is the Pirates scout who first saw Andrew play, years ago. He is sure about the kid being a potential five-tool talent but isn't quite sold on his self-confidence — until now.

Sidwell is pitching batting practice to Andrew and is startled by what he sees.

"I'm telling you, I don't want to take anything away from Rajai, but Andrew made him look like the 18-year-old high school kid," Sidwell recalls. "With 10-12 of the big guys, the upper brass standing right on top of them, that's not easy to do. He handled it like a pro, a seasoned veteran."

Sidwell will help persuade the Pirates to forget their reservations about Andrew and take him with the No. 11 overall pick in the draft.

"I was so impressed with his family," Sidwell recalls. "Especially with a high school kid, the family background is so important."

RISING UP, STAYING GROUNDED

The Indianapolis Indians, the Pirates' Class AAA affiliate, are playing the Durham Bulls, the Tampa Bay Rays' affiliate, in Durham, N.C. It is 2008, and McCutchen will start in center field for the Indians.

On the mound for the Bulls is big left-hander David Price, the No. 1 overall draft pick by the Rays in 2007. The bright futures of two franchises will soon clash.

Pat Lackey, who runs the Pirates fan blog "Where Have You Gone, Andy Van Slyke?", is in the stands. When Lackey sees McCutchen in person, he becomes skeptical. It's not that he looks smaller even than his listed height of 5 foot 10, or that his biceps don't bulge quite enough. It's just that ... this is the guy who is going to salvage the unsalvageable?

McCutchen steps to the plate in the top of the first inning, and Price looks in for the sign. Fastball. Price rears back and delivers, trying to blow one by McCutchen, and ...

Thwack!.

"Cutch flicked his wrists through the zone and sent a fly ball out to the warning track in left center," Lackey recalls. "I'm like, 'Oh, I get it! I see it now!' It was just a flyout, but now I understand why we're excited about this guy."

★★★★★★★★

Lorenzo and Petrina McCutchen are soaking up everything at their first game at PNC Park. It's 2009; that's their son, wearing No. 22 and running out to center field for the first pitch with the Pittsburgh skyline as a backdrop, a sure sign their little one is long gone from Fort Meade.

As if this day isn't special enough, it's Lorenzo and Petrina's 17th wedding anniversary. Turns out, Andrew, now 22, has something in store for them.

His first at-bat, he homers down the left field line and his parents listen to the crowd roar as he rounds the bases. In his third at-bat, after a bunt single in his second at-bat, he homers to left.

His next at-bat, he finds the left field seats again.

"I was in awe," Petrina recalls.

After McCutchen enters the dugout, the crowd demands a curtain call, and he obliges, however briefly.

He has one more trip to the plate, and the fans give him a standing ovation. Everybody in the park wants No. 4. But he grounds into a double play.

Lorenzo and Petrina McCutchen don't feel remotely short-changed.

"He gave us an awesome anniversary present," Lorenzo recalls.

In postgame interviews, McCutchen doesn't reveal that his magical night occurred on such a significant day for his family.

"It's a day I know I won't forget," he offers.

LIFE AS "THE FACE"

On Feb. 6, instead of going through his all-day workout regimen at IMG, the sports academy in Bradenton, McCutchen walks into the David L. Lawrence Convention Center in Pittsburgh to receive the Dapper Dan Sportsman of the Year award.

Pirates manager Clint Hurdle knows McCutchen would rather be preparing for spring training than making a public appearance.

The Dapper Dan is a big event, and the biggest names in Pittsburgh sports will be there — Bill Cowher, Art Rooney II, Hines Ward, to name a few. McCutchen's on-field performance and professionalism during three-plus seasons have put him in grand company.

McCutchen, wearing a sleek and shiny suit, takes the dais. He fires off the necessary thank-you's. He relays a story about playing at the Roberto Clemente baseball camp in Puerto Rico and hitting a home run. Then he goes deeper, encouraging the audience to "chase after your dreams with conviction" because "you don't have to be a great athlete to make a difference in this world."

Hurdle, watching from the podium, is blown away.

"He was so well spoken. He was entertaining. Some was scripted, some was off the cuff. It was awesome, the way he represented our organization, the city of Pittsburgh," Hurdle recalls.

★★★★★★★★

The Pirates trail the Rays 6-2 in the ninth inning of a spring training game, and McCutchen is at bat. He grounds the ball to shortstop and sprints down the first-base line, just barely beating the throw for an infield single.

After the game, Rays manager Joe Maddon wants to talk about a player on the other team.

"I want to mention their guy, McCutchen," he says. "What he did tonight, that speaks volume for all of Major League Baseball. That guy in the ninth inning of a game that means absolutely nothing hits a routine ground ball to shortstop and beats it out. I can't be more impressed. I know how good he is with everything else that he does, but for that organization to have their best player do something like that is extremely impressive. I'm a big admirer. I was, but even more so right now."

★★★★★★★★

McCutchen sits at his locker at McKechnie Field, looking at a smartphone that features the picture of him on the cover of "MLB the Show 2013" as his home screen.

A reporter wants to ask him questions about his father, about the time Lorenzo spent with him throwing batting practice, about Lorenzo leaving behind a college football career to be a more de-

voted father. He is reticent to talk about his family, but eventually relents a bit.

"He was always there," McCutchen says. "His father was in and out of his life, and I think he pretty much made a promise to himself that if he had kids he was going to be supportive, and that's what he did. I'm sure that's a lot of the reason I am who I am and I am where I'm at."

If McCutchen is trying to protect his "house," it's a worthy cause. Fort Meade today is still mostly unchanged by his growing celebrity.

Other than two signs heralding it as the home of Andrew McCutchen — one at the entrance to town and another on the front of his grandmother's store — the place is basically the same as he left it.

Visitors to the Peaceful Believers Church likely will find Lorenzo McCutchen greeting them with a smile. At the sheriff's department recruitment office, Petrina McCutchen likely will answer the phone. At the L&F Grocery, as late as 9 p.m., Andrew McCutchen's grandmother likely will be working, probably with a Pirates game on the satellite dish if the time is right. At the modest tan house where Andrew grew up, visitors will spot the sign that reads "The McCutchens" in the front yard.

"We are who we are," Petrina says. "We want home to be home. We want it to not be like a hotel or an arena of people. We want it to be comfortable and warm and inviting. I imagine if he has a good season or a better one than he had last year the demands will become more and more frequent, and he probably will need that. He'll need home."

Eight years ago, Lorenzo gave his son wings to fly, and Andrew has landed in Pittsburgh, where there is plenty of work to be done.

"He feels like he was predestined to be there," Lorenzo says. "He wants to make a difference in Pittsburgh. I think that it's important that you play where your heart is, and I think his heart is in Pittsburgh.

"When we spend time in Pittsburgh, people come up to him. … 'Andrew, can I have your autograph?' 'Can I take a picture with you?' I realize that's my son, and he's considered famous in Pittsburgh. The people love him there, and it does something to me." ∎

THE OLDER THE BETTER

Burnett, Grilli and Barmes Step Into New Roles Both On and Off the Field

By Bill Brink • March 31, 2013

It begins quietly, and on this day you probably won't be able to hear it.

Once A.J. Burnett leaves the dugout, the sellout crowd at PNC Park will roar. The chords won't poke through until he reaches the mound. The familiar cadence, repeated on a loop, da-dun-dun-dun-dun, da-dun-dun-dun-dun.

Burnett has taken the mound to Marilyn Manson's "The Beautiful People" since he was a Florida Marlin. Monday, though, he'll hear the song for the first time as an opening-day starter, the advice of his two sons ringing in his ears.

"Kick some [butt], dad," they tell him before each start. "I'll try," he responds.

Burnett's affection for Marilyn Manson was prevalent enough to make Baseball America's 359-word write-up of Burnett in 1999, when he was the Marlins' No. 1 prospect. Fourteen years, 345 games and three organizations later, the music exists for the beat.

"I don't listen much anymore," Burnett said. "I'm too old for that."

The 36-year-old Burnett has changed during his major league career. With the Pirates, he adopted the role of clubhouse elder, along with Jason Grilli and Clint Barmes. Their 34 combined years of major league service grant them the cachet to impact the clubhouse. Their success ensures that the rest of the players listen.

"He is unafraid."

Those were the final words of the "Strengths" paragraph in that Baseball America write-up. Burnett's lack of fear remains. Last September, when Brandon Phillips and Jared Hughes exchanged pleasantries after a hit-by-pitch, Burnett left the dugout and walked halfway to the baseline, alone, as backup.

He tempered his personality over 14 major league seasons. As a younger pitcher, he hadn't. He'd yell at teammates after errors, according to reports at the time. He was asked to leave the Marlins in late 2005 after criticizing his coaches and teammates.

"A.J. Burnett is a flame-throwing freak show who has no plans for the next pitch or the next day," read a portion of an *ESPN the Magazine* story about Burnett during his Marlins days.

Not only does Burnett now have a plan for the next day, it starts at sunrise. "You get here at 6:30 and A.J.'s here already," Jeff Karstens said. James McDonald is often by his side. It's probably no coincidence. After leaving the Marlins, Burnett signed with the Toronto Blue Jays, bringing him into the orbit of the king of early mornings, Roy Halladay.

"I think being around Halladay helped a lot, as far as what my purpose is," Burnett said. "It's not just to go out and pitch the best I can, but just my all-around purpose in this game.

"It took a while for me to figure that out. If I'd have been like this 10 years ago, who knows what would have happened?"

Burnett's purpose with the Pirates is more than retiring batters, eating innings, winning games. He holds sway over the clubhouse. He's not the sole source of wisdom. Barmes and Grilli play a role, as do Andrew McCutchen and others.

A.J. Burnett delivers a pitch against the Cubs on April 1 at PNC Park. The 36-year-old pitcher was the Pirates' opening-day starter in his second season in Pittsburgh.

"To pinpoint one or two guys, I don't think that's accurate," Neil Walker said. "But I don't think it's far off either."

Part of the reason the veterans earned that power so quickly was the absence of such people before their arrival.

"It's never been here before, that kind of leadership," said Karstens, who joined the organization in 2008. "If you walk in here and A.J. looks at you a certain way, you know, all right, should I be doing something?"

"When I got here, there were no set leaders," said McDonald, who joined the team at the 2010 trade deadline. "I didn't see a guy that would take charge."

Karstens, a former New York Yankee, saw how Derek Jeter and Andy Pettitte affected their teammates. When Karstens arrived at the field at 6:45 in the morning, Pettitte would be finishing his run. Burnett pairs that work ethic with the vocal aspect.

"I totally respect Paul Maholm, but was he a leader that we needed here? No. He was a good pitcher," Karstens said. "It isn't anything about him as a baseball player, it's just the kind of personality in the clubhouse."

Burnett's subtle, but important, pronouncements exempt no one. Previously, the starters not pitching on a given night sometimes watched part of that night's game from the clubhouse. Burnett, according to Karstens, ended that, starting in spring training.

"The first day, I wasn't there, but he said it," Karstens said. "Did he say it to me directly? No, but I heard it. That's all I had to do, was hear it, and I went, all right, I need to be in the dugout."

In 2012, Burnett's first season with the Pirates after being traded there by the Yankees at the start of spring training, he spoke at team meetings, including one that became public knowledge and others that didn't. He tailored his message, according to players in attendance, to fit what he determined the team needed. At times he was serious, imploring his teammates to pick up the effort. Sometimes he told them to relax and lighten up. It required a keen sense of what his teammates needed to hear. Said one player, "He's got that."

Recently Burnett's wife, Karen, found a postcard A.J. sent to his older son, A.J. Jr., about a decade ago. Technology has made keeping in touch with Karen, 12-year-old A.J. and 9-year-old Ashton easier — Ashton loves FaceTime — but that wasn't always an option, so Burnett sent postcards. The postcard Karen found had a picture of PNC Park on it. He had sent it from Pittsburgh while on a road trip.

"I happened to pick a card with Pittsburgh's stadium on it writing to my kid, and now I'm playing there and I'm with them," Burnett said. "It's kind of neat."

Because Burnett shared a rotation with Josh Beckett with the Marlins, Halladay in Toronto and CC Sabathia with the Yankees, he'll start on opening day for the first time in the park on the postcard.

WHAT'S IT LIKE?

If proceedings unfold as the opening-day crowd hopes, another song will play about three hours after Burnett takes the mound. When Grilli, at 36 a full-time closer for the first time in his career, enters from the bullpen, Pearl Jam will accompany him. He's mum on the specifics for now.

"There's no reason to go to a movie if you know the ending," Grilli said.

Grilli, like Burnett, joined the Pirates relatively recently, signing on in the summer of 2011. He spent the early portion of the season playing for Class AAA Lehigh Valley in the Philadelphia Phillies organization. Class AAA at age 34 wasn't in Grilli's initial plans.

The San Francisco Giants drafted Grilli fourth overall in 1997, and like Burnett, Grilli was the No. 1 prospect in his organization in 1998. Like Burnett, he was traded to the Marlins for a big-name pitcher — Grilli for Livan Hernandez, Burnett for Al Leiter. He and Burnett overlapped in the Marlins organization from 1999 to 2003, shortly before Burnett broke out in 2002. During that time, Grilli made six of his 16 career major league starts.

Excepting one start for Class AA Frisco in 2009, Grilli wouldn't start another professional game after 2005 and was a part of nine different organizations.

During spring training in 2010 with the Cleveland Indians, Grilli shredded part of his quadriceps and missed the season. His comeback started in Lehigh Valley.

"When I came over here, I went from being in a Triple-A situation with the IronPigs and these guys were in first place," Grilli said. "I was not going to be a part of something that they worked so hard to get to that point, and not contribute. I walked into a great situation. I was giving my all from the day I got over here because I wanted to get that respect of the guys that worked so hard to be in that situation. You want to earn the respect of your peers."

Some of the respect afforded the trio resulted from their postseason experience. Grilli played for the 2006 Detroit Tigers, who lost the World Series to the St. Louis Cardinals. Burnett won a World Series with the Yankees in 2009. Barmes played for the 2007 Colorado Rockies, who turned on the afterburners in September and blasted their way into the World Series.

"We want it so bad, we're willing to do anything," Jared Hughes said. "I'm looking at Grilli saying, 'Hey man, what's it like? What's it like in October?'"

Jason Grilli celebrates with catcher Russell Martin after pitching the ninth inning of the Pirates' 3-0 win over the Chicago Cubs on April 3, the Pirates' first win of the 2013 season. Grilli, 36, had just five career saves prior to being named the Pirates closer in 2013.

Grilli and Burnett deliver their messages in different fashions, players said. Grilli is more talkative. Burnett can be quick with a joke, but waits for teammates to seek information.

"A.J.'s kind of the guy who speaks when he needs to speak," Pedro Alvarez said. "Jason is a little bit of a chatterbox. It's a good balance of the two."

Grilli's career included more obstacles than those of Burnett or Barmes. Before his two-year, $6.75 million contract for 2013-14, Grilli's $1,875,000 million signing bonus in 1997 represented the largest payday of his career.

"If he didn't love it, there's no chance he would have stuck through it and battled through what he had to battle through," said Barmes, Grilli's roommate in Pittsburgh last season.

After he arrived, Grilli sidled up to Jeff Locke while shagging balls in the outfield, easing the nerves of the young pitcher who had yet to make his major league debut. He draws on his experience to advise younger relievers how to handle injuries or poor performance.

"We need the guys that are raw and maybe getting called up for the first time," Grilli said. "We need them just as badly as they lean on us."

As a younger player, Grilli said, he listened attentively when the veterans spoke. He kept quiet. Now he picks his spots. After the departure of Joel Hanrahan, Grilli assumed the role of the bullpen's general in addition to its elder statesman. He returned after mulling offers from the Chicago Cubs and Toronto Blue Jays offering a similar salary.

"There's a great core thing going on here, and that's a big reason why I came back," Grilli said. "That's hard to come by."

CHOOSING THEIR WORDS

Burnett won 16 games, pitched more than 200 innings and had a 3.51 ERA in 2012. Grilli struck out 90 batters in 58⅔ innings last season as a rock-solid setup man.

Barmes did not enjoy the same success in his first season with the Pirates after signing a two-year, $10.5 million contract before the 2012 season.

The Colorado Rockies drafted Barmes in the 10th round in 2000. He succeeded early, first in small pockets of at-bats in 2003-04 and later by hitting .289 with 10 home runs in 377 plate appearances in 2005, when he finished eighth in National League rookie of the year voting.

In 574 major league plate appearances between 2006-07, he hit a combined .219 with a .262 on-base percentage. He spent the majority of that 2007 season in the minors. He responded by hitting .290 with 11 home runs in 2008. From 2009-11: .242 average, .303 on-base percentage.

It was in spite of Barmes' offense that his teammates respected him. Through 70 games at the end of last June, Barmes had 44 hits in 236 plate appearances. He had a .224 on-base percentage. He struck out 55 times with four walks. Teammates credited him with preventing the struggles at the plate from affecting his defense.

"To be able to separate offense and defense is an unbelievably important thing in this game," Walker said. "It's hard to do. But it's specifically important as a middle infielder, someone that's very involved in the game. That's a very valuable lesson I learned from him."

Barmes earned his respect due to his fielding prowess and flat-line demeanor. His ultimate zone rating, a metric that attempts to quantify how many runs a player saves or allows because of his defense, ranked in the top six in the majors among shortstops in each of the past two seasons.

Barmes strives to play the game the way a professional should, and that's what he hopes to impart to the younger Pirates. He learned the craft in Colorado under Larry Walker, Vinny Castilla and Todd Helton.

"It's not like we're asking them to be anything different, or anything other than play the game the way it's supposed to be played and carry yourself," Barmes said.

The trio avoids harping on teammates, but they'll speak when they need to. Burnett and Barmes have each pulled McDonald aside to deliver messages. At times they told him he was slacking on his work. Other times, they offered advice on his mound presence. McDonald said he understood that the desire for his absolute best drove the visits. Their demeanor adds authority to their words.

"It's not meant for everybody, and that's the hard part," Karstens said. "You can't care if you're liked."

Players said Barmes sways toward Burnett's end of the spectrum. He leads by example. For the most part.

"You guys don't see the half of it with him," Walker said. "He doesn't want the limelight, he doesn't want the credit. You're not going to hear him. When he speaks, which is not very often, but when he speaks, he speaks wisely and he gets his point across and everybody listens."

PREPARING FOR BATTLE

Neither Burnett's experience nor Grilli's perseverance nor Barmes' level-headed attitude will directly contribute to the Pirates' 2013 win total. Uncertainty at the back end of the rotation, the corner outfield spots and on the bench could imperil the season. If the Pirates do play well early, they must discover a way to avoid playing their way out of contention in the second half, which they did in each of the past two seasons.

"We were upset last year," Burnett said. "We figured we're a better team. Barmie and I were talking about it. We felt like we could have done more at the end. We let these guys down at the end when it got out of control. I don't know if we did or not, but it's our responsibility."

On the rare occasion that Burnett doesn't call for Manson when he takes the field, he sometimes uses "Fever Dream," an instrumental song from the soundtrack of the movie "300." The film depicted a small contingent of Spartan warriors fighting the Persians at the Battle of Thermopylae. Burnett has a tattoo of the Spartans' leader, King Leonidas, on his left arm. He listens to the soundtrack before his starts, and likened the Spartan phalanx, a battle formation predicated upon defending one's neighbor as part of a unit, to the 25 men in the clubhouse.

"Where you're only as strong as the guy next to you," he said. "That's what the character lived by and that's how it is here, too. It's a team game. You're only as strong as your teammates. You got to pick up your teammates. And nobody wants to be that weakest link."

That's what Burnett, Grilli and Barmes try to do: prevent their teammates from being that weakest link. ■

Clint Barmes slugs a double to drive in Pedro Alvarez during the fourth inning of the Pirates' 7-1 win over the Brewers on May 16. Barmes, 34, provides a strong glove and veteran leadership.

FIRE INSIDE GRILLI FUELED RISE TO GLORY

Closer Reaches Career Pinnacle at Age 36

By Ron Cook · May 31, 2013

A fellow approached Pirates closer Jason Grilli Thursday at PNC Park and politely introduced himself before abruptly pulling back his hand just as Grilli reached to shake it. Talk about an awkward moment. Grilli didn't know what to think, the look on his face curious. "I don't want first-degree burns," the man told him. They both grinned.

Grilli is that hot.

Actually, he's hotter.

You probably know Grilli easily leads baseball in saves and was a perfect 22 for 22 in save chances going into games Thursday. You might know his strikeouts-to-walks ratio is a staggering 38-to-5 and that he is averaging 13.86 strikeouts per nine innings. But do you know only one pitcher had more saves in April and May since baseball started recognizing the stat in 1969? Danny Graves of the Cincinnati Reds had 24 in 2004 on his way to a 41-save season. None of the 10 pitchers who had 50 saves or more in a season had as many in the first two months, not even the Los Angeles Angels' Francisco Rodriguez, who had 62 in 2008 but just 21 on June 1.

Grilli's success isn't extraordinary just because he's a first-time closer. He's 36. Of the 10 pitchers with 50 saves in a season, only the Oakland Athletics' Dennis Eckersley was older when he did it. Of the 140 pitchers who had 40 or more saves in a season, only nine were 36 or older.

"I'm glad you did all that research because I don't pay any attention to it," Grilli said during a pleasant, lengthy chat in the Pirates dugout. "It goes in one ear and out the other. I know numbers are big in baseball, but I've simplified everything down to a feeling … the feeling I have when I'm on the mound. Like the guy who needs a drink, I need it. I crave it."

You saw it Tuesday night when Grilli struck out Detroit thumpers Torii Hunter, Miguel Cabrera and Prince Fielder in a one-two-three 11th inning to save the Pirates' 1-0 win. You saw it Sunday when he needed just nine pitches to retire the Milwaukee Brewers in a perfect ninth inning in a 5-4 win. You have seen it all season. Grilli retired 31 of the 35 hitters he faced in his past 11 outings. He has to be the Pirates' favorite to make the All-Star game.

First-degree burns?

How about third-degree?

"I guess if I was telling kids the significance of my story, it would be that, if you truly love what you do, don't give up on it," Grilli said. "I always wanted to be a big contributor to a team. I always wanted to do something significant. I've put in a lot of heart and perseverance to get to this point."

Let Grilli count the ways. Literally.

Jason Grilli celebrates after shutting down the Cincinnati Reds in the ninth inning on April 13 to collect his fifth save of the season. Grilli converted his first 25 save opportunities in 2013.

"Ten teams. Three surgeries. Four agents. Twelve financial advisers. Lots of cups of coffee … "

You get the idea.

Grilli hit bottom when he tore up his right knee during spring training in 2010 with the Cleveland Indians. "I was just doing my running," he said. "My kneecap ended up swinging all the way around. The guys who were running with me said it was the most disgusting sound they'd ever heard …

"[That night], I'm in a hotel room in Arizona. It took me 20 minutes to get from the bed to the toilet. I about ripped the sink out of the wall. I thought, 'This isn't supposed to happen to me.' I had a snapshot in my mind of how my career was supposed to look and that wasn't it. I knew I wasn't done with baseball."

Grilli missed the 2010 season and was stuck in Triple-A in the Philadelphia organization in 2011 when he faced a major career decision. He was married and had a 3-year-old son at the time. An offer came from Korea.

"I remember dragging my roommate — Tagg Bozied — into a laundry room at the ballpark in Scranton," Grilli said. "That was a real scary time for me. I said, 'Tagg, what should I do? Should I go to Korea?' I have to clean up his language to tell you what he told me. 'Are you kidding me? Bleep, no. If your ERA was 5 or 6, you'd be going to Korea. But your ERA is under 1. You're a big-league pitcher.' I just said thank you and gave him a big hug. I needed that confirmation at that point."

Grilli stayed with the Lehigh Valley club. The Phillies did him a favor by releasing him a month later in July so he could sign with the Pirates at the urging of manager Clint Hurdle, who had him in Colorado. Grilli finished the season strong, was a terrific eighth-inning set-up man last season and took over as closer this season after Joel Hanrahan was traded to Boston.

"People ask me what the difference is being the closer," Grilli said. "I tell them there is no difference. Instead of doing it in the eighth inning, I do it last, that's all."

Grilli made it sound simple, but it really isn't. Most baseball people will tell you there's a big difference between getting the first 24 outs of a game and the final three outs. Then again, Grilli keeps everything about baseball simple. "I try to strike out every hitter. That has to be my mindset. I have to be aggressive to be successful."

How long will it last? That seems like a fair question about the Pirates, who have a 34-20 record after beating Detroit, 1-0, in 11 innings Thursday night. It's a really fair question about Grilli, who's the oldest player on the team's active roster.

"I plan on it lasting," Grilli said. "I was on a gravel road for a long time during my career. Now, I'm on smooth pavement. I want to ride it out for as long as I can."

At that moment, it was hard to tell Grilli from a group of 8-year-old players from the Pine-Richland Baseball Association who were hanging out in the dugout. They were belly up to the railing, wide-eyed, watching Andrew McCutchen, Starling Marte and Pine-Richland's own, Neil Walker, take batting practice, soaking in all the wonder of big-league baseball.

"Those kids, they want to be us," Grilli said. "You know what the irony is? We want to be them. We are them."

That's Grilli.

A big kid in a man's body, having the time of his life. ■

Jason Grilli reacts after striking out the side against the Braves for his sixth save of the 2013 season on April 20.

COLE'S DEBUT SPECIAL FOR MANY REASONS

Young Starter Impresses in Win Over Mets

By Ron Cook · June 12, 2013

Gerrit Cole didn't make history Tuesday night. The Pirates called up phenoms before from the minor leagues. There was the redoubtable Barry Bonds in 1986. There was Jeff King, a former No. 1 overall draft choice, in 1989. There was Kris Benson, another No. 1 overall pick, in 1999. There was five-tool man Andrew McCutchen in 2009. And there was slugger Pedro Alvarez in 2010.

Cole didn't even have the Pirates' best debut, although it was plenty good in their 8-2 win against the defending world champion San Francisco Giants. Benson pitched six innings and allowed just one run and two hits in a 2-1 win against the Chicago Cubs. McCutchen singled in his first at-bat against the New York Mets' Mike Pelfrey and ended up 2 for 4 with three runs scored, an RBI, a walk and a stolen base in an 11-6 win. He's still going strong, wouldn't you agree?

But the first impression that Cole made — "You only get one," Pirates manager Clint Hurdle put it so eloquently before the game — was different from the rest. It seemed so much more significant. All of the other touted players, from Bonds to Alvarez, joined Pirates teams that were big losers with no apparent hope of winning. Cole's Pirates — we can say that now — had the third-best record (38-26) in the National League after their win, which means they would

be a playoff team if the postseason started today. Cole has a chance to be a part of something special, something even more special than just the franchise's first winning season in 21 years.

How did McCutchen put it?

"He's one of those guys who can pick up a team. He's going to bring a lot to us."

Certainly, Cole has come at the right time for the Pirates.

The team's starting pitchers had mostly decent numbers going into Tuesday night — a 22-18 record with a 3.53 ERA — but they had pitched the second-fewest innings in the National League. Then, earlier Tuesday, came word that starter Wandy Rodriguez was going on the disabled list with forearm tightness. He joins James McDonald and Jeanmar Gomez, starters who had been previously injured.

Hurdle gave the ball to Cole and asked, as he said he will do with all of the starters from this point forward, for at least seven innings. Cole came close, taking a shutout into the seventh before giving up two runs and calling it a night after 6⅓ innings that thrilled the appreciative PNC Park crowd of 30,614, which wrapped its arms around him with a standing ovation as he walked to the dugout. Cole even drove in the first two runs of the game with a second-inning single, his first hit in his year-and-a-half as a professional ballplayer. He went 0 for 6 in the minor leagues.

Gerrit Cole delivers a pitch against the Mets on July 14. Cole, the Pirates' top pick in the 2011 draft, made his major league debut in June and won his first four starts.

Hurdle was more than satisfied.

So were the other players.

"This was definitely something we needed," McCutchen said. "He's the man. Unbelievable. Unreal, man. He was everything we expected and everything he probably expected, as well …

"I can't say I'm surprised. Even in spring training, we knew what he had. He's good, man. He could have been with us from the start of the season."

Cole didn't start with the Pirates because management didn't want to start his arbitration clock. It's hard to knock that business decision. Of course, the brass will tell you Cole needed a bit more development at Class AAA Indianapolis. In any case, he seemed worth the wait Tuesday night.

The dominance by Cole, the first overall pick in the 2011 draft, was impressive, especially with his fastball, which hit 99 mph, and his control. He threw first-pitch strikes to 19 of the 27 hitters he faced. He went to two-ball counts on just five hitters, to a three-ball count on a sixth and did not walk a batter, although he hit Gregor Blanco in the second inning. He got Marco Scutaro, a .332 hitter coming in, to chase a low-and-away breaking ball and fly out harmlessly to right field with the bases loaded in the second, the first of 13 consecutive hitters he retired before Andres Torres led off the seventh with a single. The run Torres came around to score was the first Cole allowed in 25⅓ innings, going back to his time with Indianapolis.

"He pitched off his fastball," McCutchen said. "He only threw fastballs and sliders. And he pitched ahead. A lot of first-pitch strikes."

McCutchen went 2 for 3 with a double and two runs scored, but he talked as if Cole had the best at-bat of the game. The Pirates had the bases loaded in the second inning with no outs when Clint Barmes popped out to first baseman Brandon Belt in foul territory. The boos for Barmes from the big crowd turned into cheers when Cole stepped to the plate. Giants starter Tim Lincecum fooled him with a couple of sliders and put him in a hole, 0-2. But Cole hung tough, taking three consecutive balls before lining a single into the right-center gap.

"He looked like a big-league hitter, working the count like that," McCutchen said, grinning.

There were smiles all over the Pirates clubhouse after this win. Cole was the story, but he had plenty of help. The team ripped San Francisco pitching for 12 hits. Alvarez had a huge game, going 3 for 3 with a home run and three RBIs. People knock him for his .216 average, but he leads the club with 14 home runs and 37 RBIs. He has driven in 24 runs in his past 25 games. He also made a great play in the seventh inning to save a run, diving to his left to stab a shot hit by pinch-hitter Brett Pill and throwing him out.

Another Pirates starter, Charlie Morton, is expected to make his season debut Thursday night against the Giants. Morton, coming off Tommy John elbow surgery, will have to go a long way to top what Cole did.

"Today was his day," McCutchen said.

"I already can't wait to see him the next time."

A lot of us can't. ∎

Gerrit Cole delivers a pitch to San Francisco's Buster Posey during his major league debut on June 11. Cole gave up two runs in 6⅓ innings. He also collected his first major league hit.

THE POWER OF PEDRO

Home Run Swing Puts Alvarez Among Game's Top Third Basemen

By Ron Cook · June 17, 2013

The Pirates have a very good reason for staying patient with third baseman Pedro Alvarez.

"One swing … three runs," manager Clint Hurdle said.

No one on the team can change a game the way Alvarez can. His three-run home run Sunday into PNC Park's center-field shrubbery in the fifth inning after two miserable at-bats was the big blow in a 6-3 win against the Los Angeles Dodgers.

No one in the organization has Alvarez's power. "Nobody," general manager Neal Huntington confirmed. You have to love the way Hurdle put it. "When Pedro hits it, you don't have to ask if it's going out. You just wait for it to land."

That's why Pirates management is so willing — rightfully so — to stand by Alvarez despite his .213 batting average. Everyone knows he's going to fail often. "Power hitters swing and miss — a lot," Huntington said. It happened Sunday with Alvarez. In the first inning, he struck out against Dodgers starter Zack Greinke with a runner on second base. In the third, he barely made contact and hit a weak ground ball to first with the bases loaded.

You're going to get that a lot with Alvarez. Sure, it's frustrating to watch. But aren't those three-run home runs beautiful? Hurdle certainly loved the one Alvarez launched off Greinke when the score was 2-2.

"You watched us scratch and claw all weekend trying to push one [run] in," Hurdle said. "We needed someone to click one. Pedro clicked one … He stays with it. He doesn't quit on himself."

Forget about Alvarez's average for a second. Look at his power production. His 15 home runs are easily the most among National League third basemen. His 41 RBIs also lead. He has driven in 28 runs in his past 29 games.

No, Alvarez isn't as good as Detroit Tigers third baseman Miguel Cabrera, who has a chance to win a second consecutive Triple Crown this season. But Cabrera (62) and Adrian Beltre (50) of Texas Rangers are the only third basemen in the majors with more homers since the start of last season than Alvarez (45). He hit 30 a year ago.

That's the kind of offensive bang that soon will make Alvarez the really big money. He becomes eligible for the first time for salary arbitration after this season. The Pirates have his rights until after the 2016 season, when, if he isn't re-signed, he can become a free agent.

"I hope we'll be able to keep him a little longer than Cleveland kept [Jim] Thome," Huntington said.

Huntington didn't just pick future Hall of Famer Jim Thome's name out of a hat. He sees a lot of the young Thome from his early days with the Indians in Alvarez, who is in his third full big-league season.

"He would swing and miss in the zone," Huntington said. "He would swing and miss out of the zone. He would chase. There were times he looked like he didn't have a clue."

Pedro Alvarez watches his three-run homer exit PNC Park over the right-center field fence on July 3 against the Phillies. The slugging third baseman topped 30 home runs in 2012 and 2013.

Thome is unsigned and apparently finished as a player but hit 612 home runs. You might say he figured the game out. The Pirates are confident Alvarez will, as well.

"I think that will still come with the educational part of it," Hurdle said. "He'll be better as he learns the pitchers better and how they're trying to pitch him. And I think you'll see him ramp down that swing in certain situations."

Ramping down can be a good thing.

"Our challenge is to get him to understand the damage he can do with a good swing vs. the damage he can do trying to swing really hard," Huntington said.

"He is one of the elite power hitters in the game. He has unbelievable raw power."

Alvarez also has made himself into a pretty good third baseman. Again, set aside for a moment his 12 errors, the most among major league third basemen. The two plays he made Saturday in a 5-3, 11-inning loss to the Dodgers were wonderful. On the first, he lunged far to his right to stab a shot down the line and, remarkably, threw across his body with enough on the ball to get a force out at second base. On the second, he dived to his left to get the ball and throw out a runner at first.

"I can't stress enough how much pride I take in my defense," Alvarez said.

"He doesn't get enough credit for the work he's put in and the plays he makes," Huntington said. "People tend to focus on the play he didn't make rather than the three, four or five he does make that surprise you and, at times, even shock you."

Alvarez put on a show for his parents, Pedro and Luz, who were in town for the weekend. There's nothing better than a big home run for dad on Father's Day. Alvarez also had the winning hit in a 3-2 victory in New York for mom on Mother's Day. It's enough to make you curious about what he has planned for the St. Louis Cardinals Sept. 8 on Grandparents Day.

Actually, it's going to be fun to see what Alvarez does this week against the Cincinnati Reds. Chances are he will disappoint you many times, but you still won't want to take your eyes off him.

You never know when he might hit it into the Ohio River.

Who wants to miss that? ∎

Neil Walker and Garrett Jones greet Pedro Alvarez at home plate after Alvarez slugged a three-run homer against the Dodgers on June 16.

FIRST PLACE FEVER

Jose Tabata and Starling Marte race to celebrate with Jordy Mercer after Mercer's game-winning single in the 11th inning lifted the Pirates past the Mets on July 12.

BEST MARK LOOKS GOOD, BUT ROAD STILL IS LONG

Pirates Head into July Sporting Baseball's Best Record

By Jenn Menendez · June 30, 2013

The Pirates woke up Saturday to the best record in baseball: 49-30.

That view from the top perch in the National League Central Division, a game ahead of the St. Louis Cardinals, put the Pirates smack in the middle of their best season in some 20 years.

Yet manager Clint Hurdle refused to get ahead of himself, saying there's a long way to go before those numbers really add up.

"I think you've got to acknowledge it's the best season we've had in 20 years, so far," Hurdle said. "Be easy to please, hard to satisfy. The players are that way. I'm that way. Yes we're happy with what we've done. But we understand there's many more miles on this road to travel. The lessons we've learned from the past two years, I think, are instrumental and going to be strength for us moving forward."

Hurdle said the team will continue to control the grind, eliminate distractions and get a little better each day.

"Lastly, they don't break trophies in half. They never have, they never will," Hurdle said. "So we've got to continue to believe in the process of what we're building here and acknowledge the fact it's gotten us to a workable place. But there's more out there."

Outfielder Andrew McCutchen, who has a hit in six of his past seven games, said there was no extra spring in his step when he woke up to sole possession of first place.

"Every game counts, but it's not the end of the season," McCutchen said. "A record can fluctuate just like stats do, up and down.

"We're not really worried about it. We've still got a lot of games to play. That's something we can assess at the end of the season."

Hurdle was briefly incredulous when he remarked on some of the things he said he hears from the public when he's about town.

"You know how many times I still hear it? 'What's going to happen late?' I don't know, watch. Stay tuned," Hurdle said of fans wondering if there will be another collapse. "I believe I know what's going to happen, but you know there's people who are never going to believe. Actually, I think there's some people here who hope we don't pull it off. That sounds crazy, doesn't it?

"I can't control other people's emotions. I just kind of enjoy the ride, the perspective of it all going on, and know there's going to be a day when this city will be rocking and people are going to be happy and it's going to be all good. That's what I believe. ... Somebody's got to hold the wheel." ∎

Fans on top of PNC Park's outfield rotunda wave a flag during the Pirates' win over the Milwaukee Brewers on June 28. By late June, the Pirates were leading the National League East and had the best record in the major leagues.

IT'S TIME TO EMBRACE THE PITCHING

Staff Among Baseball's Best

By Ron Cook · July 12, 2013

Former Pirates general manager Dave Littlefield had a curious way of looking at baseball. Please, hold the jokes. Before each series, Littlefield would compare his team's starting pitchers to the opponent's starters. "We have an edge with Kris Benson against [Jimmy] Haynes," he would say. "It's a toss-up with Kip Wells and [Ryan] Dempster. I like Josh Fogg over [Jimmy] Anderson. This should be a good series for us."

Littlefield said just that before the season-opening series in 2003 in Cincinnati. The Pirates swept the Reds. Unfortunately, for Littlefield and his team, there were too many Ryan Vogelsong vs. CC Sabathia and Jeff D'Amico vs. Curt Schilling matchups later in the summer. Those Pirates finished 75-87.

This is just a guess, but Littlefield probably would love generally managing the 2013 Pirates.

All of us have done much moaning about the team's often-lame offense. The complaints have not been without justification. The Pirates need to get more hitting from first base, second base, shortstop and, if Jose Tabata isn't the long-term answer, right field. They struggle mightily to score runs.

But today doesn't seem like the right day for fretting. The Pirates will take a 54-36 record into their game tonight at PNC Park against the New York Mets, the start of their final series before the All-Star break. Can we step back and take a moment to appreciate the pitching staff? It has been wonderful.

Its 3.09 ERA was the best in baseball going into the games Thursday. Its .225 batting average against was the lowest in the game. Its 1.18 WHIP was tied with the Cincinnati Reds for the best in baseball. All of that is beyond wonderful.

The pitchers are why the Pirates aren't going to collapse again in the second half. They are why the team will end its horrendous streak of 20 consecutive seasons. They might even be good enough to get the Pirates to the postseason for the first time since 1992. They held a 7½-game lead over the Washington Nationals for the final playoff spot going into Thursday.

The bullpen has been the best in baseball. No less than Detroit Tigers manager Jim Leyland said that earlier in the season. Many nights, Mark Melancon and Jason Grilli turn a game into a seven-inning game. The Pirates are 41-2 when they lead after seven.

But it is the starting pitchers who deserve the most credit. They are without three of the five men in their season-opening rotation — Wandy Rodriguez, James McDonald and Jonathan Sanchez — and didn't have a fourth — A.J. Burnett — for a month. They didn't just survive. They have thrived. They have allowed three or fewer earned runs in 24 of their past 25 starts.

Francisco Liriano has been a revelation since joining the rotation May 11. A 9-3 record. A 2.00 ERA, which is second lowest in baseball behind the Los Angeles Dodgers' Clayton Kershaw among regular starters. A string of 10 of 12 starts in

Francisco Liriano throws out a Giants runner at first base on June 12. Liriano signed with the Pirates as a free agent in February 2013 and emerged as the team's No. 1 starter.

which he allowed two earned runs or fewer. He has been amazing.

Jeff Locke also has had surprising success. He went 16 consecutive starts without losing before a 2-1 loss Monday night to the Oakland Athletics. That defeat might have been his most impressive outing; he gave up two runs and three hits in seven innings. His 2.15 ERA is the third best in baseball.

Burnett returned to the rotation Sunday after a month off because of a calf injury. He threw five strong innings against the Chicago Cubs and appears ready for a good second half.

Phenom Gerrit Cole has gone at least six innings in four of his six starts and allowed three or fewer runs in each. The Pirates should send him back to the minor leagues today or Saturday. Not because he has pitched poorly; he allowed two runs and five hits in a 2-1 loss Tuesday night to the Athletics. Because he could stay on a five-day schedule, something he can't do with the Pirates, who are off four days next week for the break. And, just as important, because the Pirates could slow his Super 2 arbitration clock and save the franchise millions down the road. Cole could return for an important series against the Nationals July 22-25 when the Pirates will need a fifth starter.

Charlie Morton is the weak spot in the rotation, but he has made just five starts — one was cut to two innings because of a rain delay — since returning from Tommy John elbow surgery. There is no reason to think he won't get stronger with each outing, perhaps starting tonight when he gets the ball against the Mets.

If Morton fails, Jeanmar Gomez has shown he can give the Pirates at least five good innings. His WHIP is lower than that of Liriano, Locke, Cole and Morton.

We're talking talent and depth.

That doesn't mean you are wrong if you are skeptical. You earned that right last season after watching the Pirates go 16-36 down the stretch, one of the worst collapses in baseball history. Their team ERA was 3.47 before the All-Star break, 4.29 after. No one represented that failure more than McDonald, who followed a superb first half with a pathetic second.

But it's hard to imagine any of the starters falling apart like that this season. Not Liriano, who often was inconsistent with the Minnesota Twins and Chicago White Sox. Not Locke and Cole, who are mere babies in a baseball sense. Certainly not Burnett.

Worry about the Pirates hitters tomorrow.

Enjoy the pitchers today.

They are a special group. ∎

Jason Grilli celebrates after striking out the Dodgers' Mark Ellis to collect his 24th save of the season on June 14. Grilli anchored one of baseball's top bullpens in 2013.

FINALLY ... THE RIGHT MIX?

Small Moves Prove to Be the Magic Elixer Pirates Have Been Seeking

By Bill Brink · July 14, 2013

They came from unlikely places. One was on his third organization and found himself sent off the 40-man roster in February. Another was the return when the Pirates traded Quincy Latimore, he of the .253 career average in 2,943 minor league plate appearances. A third entered spring training with his non-pitching arm immobilized in a brace. Still another barely eked his way into the rotation.

The men who comprise the Pirates pitching staff coalesced into the unit that has spearheaded the team's charge toward its first playoff berth since 1992. Entering the final game today before the All-Star break, the Pirates are 56-36 and even with the St. Louis Cardinals atop the National League Central Division. This is not a drill.

"I feel like a proud father," said Mark Melancon, the Pirates' dominant set-up man. "It's really cool."

Neither the pitching staff nor the record can erase the events of the previous two seasons, when similar — though less drastic — stretches of good performance gave way to poor play in the second half that extended the franchise's stretch of consecutive losing seasons to 20. The players will tell you they don't care. Thinking about 2012 can't help them win this year, they say. Their manager agrees, to a point.

Clint Hurdle believes it is important to remember what happened in the past to avoid similar results in the future.

Whatever their view, they're here now, poised to make a legitimate run at the playoffs. For the time being, they are no longer an anomaly, no longer a statistical quirk awaiting correction.

"You take the small victories and you try to enjoy the small steps along the way," general manager Neal Huntington said, "but we've still got some big steps in front of us."

Here's how they're doing it.

In 2009, with the Pirates on their way to a 62-99 record and a last-place finish in the NL Central, Huntington, then in his second season as GM, decided it was time to trade Nate McLouth.

When Huntington made the move, he chose a deal that netted a 21-year-old left-handed pitcher with clean mechanics and a good breaking ball. Now, Jeff Locke is an All-Star. His 2.15 ERA ranked second only to Cy Young winner Clayton Kershaw entering the weekend's games. He doesn't strike many guys out (6.0 per nine innings) and walks a few too many (3.9 per nine), but in 18 starts this year, he has kept opposing batters from hitting the ball very hard.

"It's been fun to watch him develop into what our scouts said he could be," Huntington said.

James McDonald delivers a pitch against the Giants in July 2012. McDonald, who won 12 games for the Pirates in 2012, was 2-2 in April 2013 before going on the disabled list with a shoulder injury.

Specifically, Locke has kept the ball in the park. The six home runs he allowed in 109 innings entering today's game matched his total in 34⅓ innings in 2012. He has allowed more than three earned runs only twice and has finished six innings in 11 of his 18 starts.

"I think every once in a while there's a little reality check, but nothing you didn't know you could do," Locke said. "You just hadn't done it yet."

Locke and his counterparts have posted a 3.10 team ERA this season that ranks as the best mark in the majors. Their 3.37 runs allowed per game also leads the majors.

This season did not begin well for Francisco Liriano. A broken right humerus, which he said he suffered slamming his arm into a door to scare his children on Christmas Day, lowered what could have been a two-year, $12.75 million contract to a one-year deal with only $1 million guaranteed. A vesting option and bonuses allowed him to make more, but starting the season on time was out.

Once the arm healed, there were control problems to work through. Liriano walked five batters per nine innings in each of the previous two seasons. He was well removed from a solid season in 2010 and a spectacular sophomore campaign in 2006 that ended prematurely due to elbow surgery.

Liriano figured it out. He has walked 3.3 batters per nine innings and struck out 80 in 76⅔ innings, winning nine games despite not starting for the Pirates until May 11.

"He made the comment to me, 'I found a way to settle down when I do get a runner on base,'" Hurdle said. "It used to be, 'When I'd get runners on base, I really kind of amped up. I overpitched, which became more problematic. I didn't have the fastball command that I have now in those situations. Probably wasn't as sharp with my breaking stuff or as effective with my changeup. I just overthrew.' He found a way to back off."

Liriano closed the first half well, allowing two runs in a complete game against the Chicago Cubs, and pitching seven scoreless innings to stop a four-game losing streak and beat the Oakland Athletics.

"He's been able to command his fastball and be aggressive in his zone with his fastball better, which is what really sets him up for success," Huntington said.

When Jeanmar Gomez found out he was traded from the Cleveland Indians to the Pirates, he got a trio of phone calls: Huntington, Hurdle and pitching coach Ray Searage.

"They said, 'Hey, welcome to the Pittsburgh Pirates,'" Gomez said. " 'Welcome aboard. We'll see you in spring training.'"

Gomez had a 5.18 ERA in 206⅔ innings with the Indians. He has helped the Pirates overcome numerous injuries to the rotation, amassing a 2.65 ERA in 51 innings split between starting and relief work. His moment: Seven scoreless innings May 28 on the road against the Detroit Tigers, before Neil Walker's 11th-inning home run to give the Pirates a win.

The pitching staff has done a good portion of its work without James McDonald, who suffered from ineffectiveness and a loss of velocity before shoulder pain sent him to the disabled list in early May. Forearm problems have sent Wandy Rodriguez to the DL, and Charlie Morton did not return until mid-June from his 2012 elbow surgery.

Outwardly, the pitchers don't acknowledge their stellar performance.

"Me, I don't pay attention," Gomez said. "I try to go game to game. Today we're facing Oakland. OK.

"We have the best record — OK. It's a number. We play today's game. We focus on today. We have to make quality pitches."

The Pirates tried to acquire Vin Mazzaro when he began his career in the A's organization. They tried again when he went to Kansas City.

"When he became available, we thought it'd be an interesting get for us, a guy with some upside and a guy with a good arm that could fit in a multi-inning role out of the chute and maybe mature with something more than that," Huntington said.

Mazzaro's Pirates career could have been dead in the water.

Jason Grilli wraps his arm around catcher Russell Martin after the Pirates' closer notched his 16th save of the season against the Brewers on May 15.

They outrighted him to Class AAA Indianapolis to make room for Liriano in February. The bullpen needed help in April, though, and up he came. He had allowed 13 earned runs in 40⅓ innings entering the weekend for a bullpen that ranks second in the majors with a 2.86 ERA.

"I guess in the beginning, when I was in Indy, I kind of followed a little bit," Mazzaro said.

"The bullpen's doing an outstanding job. The starters are doing great. We're just coming in and pitching effective, pounding the zone, getting the job done."

Any discussion of the pitching staff must include A.J. Burnett, the don of the rotation, and Jason Grilli, who at 36 made his first All-Star team and leads the NL with 28 saves. Top prospect Gerrit Cole came up and reeled off four wins in a row.

With a league-leading ERA comes a league-leading batting average on balls in play. The Pirates' .264 BABIP is the lowest in the majors. Though good pitching mitigates that to some degree, a correction closer to the .290-.300 league average is likely.

That will make it harder for the Pirates pitching staff to compensate for the team's offense, which ranks 25th in the majors with 3.86 runs per game and 21st with a .309 on-base percentage. The July 31 trade deadline, by which point the Pirates could try to upgrade the offense, looms.

"We have room for improvement," Hurdle said. "We have people there that are capable of doing, I think, a little bit more than what they have. I don't think we have anybody here exceeding expectations and we've got a few who are probably underachieving a little bit what we believe they are able to do."

How do the pitchers continue their success?

"Not change anything," Liriano said. "Try to do the same thing we've been doing in the first half."

"Continuing to trust our defense, continue to believe this offense is going to get rolling, essentially keep doing what they've been doing to get here," Huntington said.

"Don't change anything," Mazzaro said.

That, it appears, is the formula: Don't deviate from the process in the first half so they can turn the tables on the results in the second. ∎

A.J. Burnett pitches against the Mets on July 13. The veteran right-hander allowed two runs in 5⅔ innings as the Pirates moved into a first-place tie atop the National League Central division.

BASEBALL SUDDENLY SERIOUS IN CITY AGAIN

Are Fans Trying to Reorient Themselves to a Winning Team?

By J. Brady McCollough · July 14, 2013

Matt Light knows only one Pittsburgh. His city has well-regarded hospitals and universities, affordable housing and an abundance of cheap tickets to professional baseball games.

It has been a good life. As an adolescent in West View, he strove to be a class clown. He also attended about 20 Pirates games a year. Turned out, those interests would go hand in hand. When Light decided to start doing stand-up comedy a few years ago, he didn't have to think too hard about the right topic to use as an opener.

Light, 24, has a dark edge to his humor. He would have to reel audiences into his routine with something safe that was guaranteed to engage any Pittsburgher. It went something like this:

He walks on stage to minimal applause. Come on, you guys sound like PNC Park! How's everyone doing tonight?! Louder applause. The Pirates have been so bad for so long, the only time the game is exciting for a fan is during the fifth-inning pierogi race. It's the only time your guy has a chance of winning. … The promotions are stupid, because, whoever that bobblehead is, he's going to be traded next week. … Here's what they need to do: At the beginning of the game, announce 'FANS, TAKE OUT YOUR TICKET. IF YOU ARE IN SECTION 103, ROW 7, SEAT 3, CONGRATULATIONS, YOU ARE NOW THE STARTING

PITCHER FOR THE PITTSBURGH PIRATES!'"

Light wrote this opener believing that he'd be able to use it into eternity. Pirates jokes have become the lifeblood of Pittsburgh's self-deprecating humor. When in doubt of what to say in this town, grumble something about those lousy Buccos, their lousy owner or two decades of futility, and you'll fit right in. But Light, a lifelong Pirates fan, has noticed a change in dynamics, and frankly, it's not good for business.

The Pirates are 56-36, firmly in a position for a playoff spot this coming October, and Light has had to write a new opener.

"I haven't been able to use my Pirates stuff this year," he said, "and it [stinks] because honestly out of all my jokes that's the most reliable. It's like that pain that everybody in the city has, but you can laugh at it now because it's been so long it's pathetic. Now people are like, 'This team's turned it around. This is it.'"

Baseball is suddenly serious again in Pittsburgh. As the All-Star break begins with the Pirates eyeing meaningful September games for the third consecutive season, it is no laughing matter for the North Side faithful.

So many being so eager to take the plunge has challenged folks like Light, who have made a living on the Pirates as a laughingstock. Sean Collier, a local comedian who works at *Pittsburgh Magazine,* has been using the Pirates as the closer to his routine for a few years now.

Pirates fans celebrate in the stands at PNC Park during the second game of a doubleheader against the Cardinals on July 30. The two wins gave the Pittsburgh a 1½-game lead over St. Louis in the National League Central.

"I have a joke about how the Pirates have made me believe in miracles more than anybody else," said Collier, 28, "because if I can go to the ballpark for 20 years and think something good might happen, clearly, anything is possible for me."

Collier is still using that one, but he admits it's no longer connecting.

The citizenry appears ready for one of Pittsburgh's last bastions of ineptitude to fall, and, if it does, here's fair warning: You may not recognize your city.

LOYALTY TO BASEBALL

Lush green ivy covers the tall red brick wall in Oakland near Schenley Park, helping to create an accurate rendering of old Forbes Field but at the same time camouflaging a key relic of a town's sporting foundation from the near-constant car and foot traffic.

Pittsburgh baseball has a grand history, and you know that when you see 78-year-old Herb Soltman regaling four visitors in what was once right-center field on a recent afternoon. Soltman was 25 and in attendance when Bill Mazeroski's home run cleared this wall in 1960, leading the Pirates to a World Series championship over the vaunted New York Yankees. Now, Mr. Soltman comes back here every year as president of the Game 7 Gang, to relive a time when the Pirates, not the Steelers, were the top source of civic pride.

These men came to the wall as part of a pilgrimage, a four-city baseball road trip. They hailed from Virginia, Ohio and Arizona, and they felt lucky to meet Mr. Soltman, who has defined himself by the unbridled happiness he felt as a much younger man.

"Isn't that cool!" Fred Hill said to Soltman, who was flipping through a photo album. "Is that Mazeroski?"

The middle-aged men are excited about the Pirates' recent success and, despite being Cubs, Braves, Indians and Diamondbacks fans, will be rooting for Pittsburgh in the coming months because, hey, what a story!

Back in the day, though, the Pirates didn't need anyone's sympathy. Nationally, they were about the only thing anybody knew about Pittsburgh other than it was a murky gray steel town with a sorry professional football team.

In Western Pennsylvania, Pirates fandom meant more than cheering the hometown team. The blue-collar men who settled here after traveling from faraway lands used the Pirates to feel American.

John Stanko's grandfather, Alex Crouse, immigrated from Ukraine and worked in a coal mine outside of Latrobe in the 1950s. He didn't speak much English, but he'd learn to understand the cultural language of choice.

"I remember him sitting on the porch outside with a fly swatter and the radio on, listening to every pitch of every game," said Stanko, 63, pastor of the Allegheny Center Alliance Church on the North Side. "That's what he lived for."

Richard "Pete" Peterson's father was a car mechanic by trade, his mother a waitress. His family didn't have much living on the South Side, but they had baseball. The sport provided them with generational heroes: Honus Wagner, Pie Traynor, then Bill Mazeroski, and, eventually, Roberto Clemente and Willie Stargell.

"For working-class families, the Pirates sort of defined the character of the city for us," said Peterson, who has written several books about Pirates history. "That gave us a focus for our lives."

Stanko and Peterson came up in different parts of the city but shared a rooting experience: Knowing from year to year that your favorite Pirates would be there. Yes, the only big trades in those days involved your buddies and a pack of baseball cards.

The Pirates were dominant in the '70s, right along with the emerging Steelers, bringing home World Series titles in 1971 and 1979. In the '80s, though, free agency began, allowing salaries to start their exponential climb. The Pirates drafted Barry Bonds and built a winner again under manager Jim Leyland from 1990-92, but everybody knew 1992 was going to be it for Bonds — and, likely, winning.

When Sid Bream's slide completed the Braves' ninth-inning comeback over the Pirates in Game 7 of the National League Championship Series that fall, Stanko, then 42, stood in front of the television set and cried.

"Baseball may never be back in Pittsburgh," Stanko remembers saying.

Never mind that he was a man of faith.

CREATING SEPARATION

No matter how big a Pirates fan you were, there came a point when you had to think about self-preservation. No, this would not be the year, nor the next, nor the next. There would never, ever, be a year.

When Pittsburghers took themselves out to the ballgame, they went thinking more so about peanuts and Cracker Jack and, once the team moved into PNC Park, that majestic view of a city on the rise.

"With the Pirates, you had to divorce yourself," says Steve Hansen, a former Pittsburgh radio disc jockey who lives on the North Side. "They're still your team, but you have to divorce yourself from caring too much, because then that makes you a loser. You kid about it. They were a joke because that's how you maintained sanity in the relationship. I like them, but I know that they [stink]. It's OK. I'm not a loser. They're a loser."

Teammates mob Andrew McCutchen after McCutchen hit a single in the bottom of the ninth inning to beat the Philadelphia Phillies in April 2012. Pirates fans have flocked to PNC Park to enjoy McCutchen and the Pirates' other young stars.

They were the ones who had to grab the national spotlight all those years by performing the absurd, like then-Pirate Randall Simon bumping a woman dressed in a sausage costume with a bat in Milwaukee's Miller Park in 2003, or, years later, by losing to those same Brewers 20-0.

There were some fans who just couldn't cut the cord, no matter how hard they tried. Matt Wein, 30, of Squirrel Hill would walk away from the team for weeks or months but always came back, not fully invested but somehow unable to remove himself from the inevitable further wreckage of his soul.

Wein was old enough in 1992 to know what winning baseball felt like.

The Pirates got their hooks into him more than the back-to-back Stanley Cup champion Penguins and the early Bill Cowher Steelers.

"I've long said that, before I'm an American or Jewish or anything else I'm a Pittsburgher," Wein said, "and second to Pittsburgher is I'm a Pirates fan."

Wein has bled so much that he's become protective of his pain. He wants people to know that he's been loyal through it all, not some bandwagon jumper. A few years ago, he bought the jersey of former Pirate pitcher Ryan Vogelsong, a failed pitcher in Pittsburgh during 2001-06 who cruelly went on to help the Giants win a World Series in 2011, because wearing it would show the authenticity of his sadness.

"The thing I've come to enjoy about being a Pirates fan is that you're a member of a very small group," Wein said, "and there's an exclusivity to it. By wearing a Ryan Vogelsong jersey around, I get the most fantastic looks. I was a Pirate fan before it was cool."

Even in the leanest years, there was a unique enjoyment to being a Pirates fan. Wein came to care more about the intricacies of the game than the actual results — "If I were a person who let the Pirates losing just ruin my day, I would have killed myself years ago," he joked — and often took satisfaction from the smallest of victories.

Long-suffering Pirates fans, in this weird way, had the opportunity to gain a greater perspective on life by simply finding a way to appreciate their lemon that would never make lemonade.

"It's made me a little bit more optimistic," said Collier, the comedian. "If I lived in Boston, and I bought tickets to a game, I would be expecting them to win, and I would be [mad] if they lost if I spent that money. But being a Pirates fan, for the majority of my life, if I'm being honest with myself, I'm walking into the park thinking that they're probably going to lose. If they win, that's like a bonus for me. I think that's the joy of loving a bad team."

CHANGE ON THE WAY?

There is no joy in Mudville, though, as Ernest Thayer pointed out in his classic 1888 poem "Casey at the Bat," nor in any other 'ville that is cheering a team playing under the weight of expectations.

With this intrepid bunch of Pirates reaching the best record in baseball halfway through the season at 21 games over .500 on June 30, their fans are having to remember what was meant by the phrase "agony of defeat."

"It's really disorienting," Hansen said. "Because with the Pirates, summertime rolls around, and it's a much more social experience than a baseball experience. There's no urgency. And now it's, like, real baseball, and hits and runs have consequences. I have to really reorient myself.

"When you're playing for something, the pitch comes, and you hold your breath. It's a ball, it's a strike, you relax for that second, and you're back at it. For 20 years in Pittsburgh, it's never been like that."

For those like Hansen, it is reorientation. But for the city's youth, it's simply orientation. If you're younger than 27 or 28, you've probably never known what it's like to cheer winning baseball here.

Andrew Goleman is 21 years old, a native of Squirrel Hill and a student at Temple University. He was born a few months before Mr. Bream's slide. His family had season tickets at Three Rivers Stadium but stopped once the team moved to PNC Park and continued the losing. Still, he never stopped caring, never stopped hoping to say those four special words and mean them:

"This is the year," Goleman will tell you now.

Say that he's right. Would one year of playoff baseball turn off the nozzle on Pirates jokes, or would the well stay full until the franchise maintains a solid footing?

"If they can sustain and compete for a stretch, it will change the culture of a generation," said John Supp, 43, who hosts several large Pirates tailgates a year. "You will see a Pittsburgh where you don't hear those jokes or grumblings. As long as the gap between this and the next cycle isn't 20 years."

Pittsburgh has never had all three major professional sports teams playing at a high level at the same time. Goleman would like to see it. Now.

"I can't imagine it, how electric the city would be," Goleman said. "It really can be one of the best sports cities in the world if the Pirates can start winning."

This afternoon at PNC Park, they'll get another chance, one of 162, and if the Pirates lose to the Mets, you're going to feel something stirring in your gut. It's not going to be laughter, not anymore. ■

Andrew McCutchen received a pie in the face after hitting a walk-off home run in the bottom of the 12th inning to beat the Milwaukee Brewers on May 14, 2013. Pirates fans have embraced the talented team that doesn't take itself too seriously.

DRIVEN TO SUCCEED

Setup Man Melancon, Fellow All-Star Pirates Want Much More from Season

By Bill Brink · July 16, 2013

Due to the short notice of Mark Melancon's All-Star selection, he traveled to Citi Field via ground transportation.

And loved it.

"It was better than flying because I got to relax, I got to talk," Melancon said of the six-hour drive with his family. "It was actually a really neat experience."

Melancon was the fifth and final Pirates player selected to participate in the All-Star festivities and the game tonight at Citi Field. National League manager Bruce Bochy selected setup man Melancon to replace Jeff Locke, who missed his start Sunday because of tightness in his lower back.

Melancon deserved the invitation. He has walked four and allowed four earned runs in 44⅓ innings this season in addition to striking out 46.

"It's a very big deal, and I'm so glad that Melancon, they got it right," said fellow All-Star Jason Grilli, the recipient of many save opportunities in games that Melancon has kept close.

As excited as Grilli was to join Melancon, Locke, Andrew McCutchen and Pedro Alvarez as the Pirates' representation, he credited the rest of his bullpen with some of his success and spoke highly of the impact his season has had on his teammates.

"Some of the texts I've got from my teammates, even when I was here, I was in tears [Sunday] night," he said. "I think the biggest accolade beyond being named an All-Star is you get the respect and the admiration and the well-wishes from your teammates. You get the respect of your peers, you can take that to the bank."

The Pirates faced familiar questions Monday, held in the open-air Jackie Robinson rotunda. MLB employees brought the players towels to help them combat the mid-90-degree heat.

Grilli discussed his long journey to becoming a shutdown closer and first-time All-Star at 36; Alvarez, talked about his improvement since May and performing in the Home Run Derby in his hometown; Melancon, spoke about the Pirates' playoff chances.

"That's an expectation for sure," Melancon said.

"If we don't get there, that would be devastating. It's how far we're going to get in the playoffs is what we're talking about."

Alvarez received a barrage of questions about the Derby, including his thoughts about the PNC Park crowd's hostility toward National League Derby captain David Wright during the weekend series against the New York Mets.

"The guy obviously doesn't deserve that," Alvarez said. "That's that."

McCutchen, playing in his third All-Star Game, gave the others the finer points of the events — where to be, what to wear, etc.

Jeff Locke earned his sixth win of the 2013 season on June 14, shutting out the Dodgers on two hits through seven innings. Locke was named to the National League All-Star team after earning eight wins in his first 10 decisions.

Melancon had breakfast with his extended family, who flew in from out of town.

Locke wanted to make sure he got to meet Los Angeles Dodgers pitching ace Clayton Kershaw, the one man Locke pegged as a must.

"I met him on a bus," Locke said. "I went to go introduce myself and he was like, 'Hey Jeff.' I was like, no way. That's the coolest thing in the world.

On the stage for all to see, the Pirates' representatives said they weren't focused on what the exposure could do for themselves or for a team that, at 56-37, has surprised many fans and observers.

"I don't think we're trying to make a name for ourselves individually here," Melancon said.

"What I've gathered in the clubhouse and feel in the clubhouse is the Pirates are a team group all the way."

"We focus on ourselves," Alvarez said.

"We know what we have in front of us. We're so invested in one another that we just worry about what we can do to win some ballgames.

"One of the biggest factors is not worrying about external distractions."

Even on the high note of the good first-half record and the All-Star representation, McCutchen noted that the Pirates weren't done.

"I feel like we're only getting better, we're only going to get better going into the second half," he said.

"It's not, we've reached our plateau. We did good, now we go out there just to continue working and do even better as a team."

The players invited to New York, Melancon said, represented that.

"It shows the talent we have on our team," he said. "The production that we're getting is not a fluke, it's for real." ■

Pedro Alvarez hits a two-run homer against the Braves in the second inning on April 19, 2013. The ball traveled 430 feet. Alvarez's team-leading 24 home runs in the first half earned the third baseman a spot on the National League All-Star team.

BRING IT ON

For Huntington, Now Is Not Right Time to Crow

By Ron Cook · July 19, 2013

Pirates general manager Neal Huntington insists he isn't tempted. He swears he has no desire to grab a microphone, climb to the top of the PNC Park mound and scream to the world, "Look at me now!" It doesn't matter that Huntington's team, finally, looks as if it could be a big winner this season, his sixth on the job. So what if the Pirates are 56-37 heading into the second half? Huntington says he won't gloat. That goes beyond the obvious, that much baseball remains to be played, 69 games beginning with one tonight in Cincinnati against the Reds. "They don't celebrate half-seasons," Huntington said. But there is more to it than that. Huntington knows he can be regarded as an idiot again real soon. "No question. I know how quickly that can happen."

Huntington is under tremendous pressure as the trade deadline approaches at the end of the month. Does he do nothing and stick with a team that has been surprisingly successful? Does he try to make it better by adding a starting pitcher, a bat, even a bench player? Does he give up a big part of the franchise's future by trading a top prospect to make a major acquisition — maybe a high-priced rental player — and take an all-in shot at a championship this season?

Easy questions to ask.

Hard questions to answer.

"We've got to be open-minded to anything," Huntington said.

The guess here is Huntington will make a move or two but not a major trade. He acknowledged, "This is a club we believe in … Today really means a lot." But he said he isn't inclined to "sell out for the present" unless a trade really makes sense. It seems unlikely he will deal any of his top prospects, notably pitcher Jameson Taillon, outfielder Gregory Polanco and shortstop Alen Hanson.

"The organizations that sustain success have three-quarters of their eye on the moderate-to-long-term future and one-quarter of their eye on the present," Huntington said. "There are no exact percentages for that and there is no perfect model, but successful organizations always are cognizant of the future. It's my job to make sure this isn't a one-and-done situation."

I've blamed Huntington for just about everything during the past five years, but I have a hard time blaming him for that strategy.

It makes perfect sense.

The team Huntington has built might be good enough — as is — to win the National League Central Division or at least get a wild-card spot. The pitching staff has been the best in baseball and shouldn't fold the way it did last season. Huntington's offseason moves to bring in Francisco Liriano, Mark Melancon, Jeanmar Gomez and Vin Mazzaro have turned out to be wonderful, trumping his unsuccessful decisions to sign Jonathan Sanchez and Jose Contreras and give a new contract to Jeff Karstens. Pitching and defense can carry a team a long way, even a team that often is light on offense.

"It's not that we don't have any weaknesses, but we feel like we don't have any desperate weaknesses," Huntington said.

That won't stop Huntington from working the phones. There's no time to enjoy that terrific record, although he said he does try "to celebrate the small successes along the way." Certainly, there is no time to snipe back at his many critics, who have ripped him for everything from his trades and acquisitions to the way the organization develops its young players. Remember the hysteria over his use of Navy SEALs training last fall?

"I'm just thrilled for the fans and the people I work with," Huntington said.

Pirates manager Clint Hurdle (left) talks with Neal Huntingon during batting practice at the Pirates' spring training facility in Bradenton, Florida. Huntington was named the Pirates' general manager in September 2007 and is credited with building the franchise's first winning team in more than 20 years.

Huntington signed a three-year contract extension in September 2011 with a club option for 2015. There was no guarantee he would last after the Pirates collapsed last season, finishing 16-36 after being 63-47 Aug. 9. General managers in a lot of cities don't get a sixth year. But owner Bob Nutting stuck with Huntington. Today, at least, Nutting looks pretty smart.

"Do I feel fortunate? I feel fortunate that they gave me this opportunity in the first place," Huntington said. "In terms of self-doubt, I believe in the people I work with and the way we do things. I'm a process-creates-results guy. I believe in our process …

"We wanted to win in Year 3 and Year 4 and Year 5. But it's not easy turning a major league baseball team around. It's not easy turning a major league organization around. In baseball, it takes more players and takes more time."

The job isn't finished, of course. Huntington knows that. The Pirates are sitting in a nice spot, trailing the first-place St. Louis Cardinals by one game in the division and holding a four-game lead over the Reds for the first wild card and a nine-game lead over the Washington National for the second. But there's no trophy presentation scheduled yet.

"They don't celebrate half-seasons."

"It's a big challenge to get here, but it's an even bigger challenge to stay here," Huntington said.

"We want to put ourselves in position to celebrate a full season and, hopefully, a postseason."

Huntington has given the Pirates a chance. Even his toughest critics have to admit that. ■

THE WORD: MELANCON JUST AS GOOD

Pirates Remain Confident Despite Losing Dominant Closer Grilli

By Ron Cook · July 24, 2013

The mood in the Pirates clubhouse Tuesday was decidedly upbeat. Many of the players had talked with closer Jason Grilli earlier in the day before he returned to Pittsburgh to be examined by team orthopedist Dr. Patrick DeMeo and found him to be surprisingly optimistic. "We don't think it's the end of the world," general manager Neal Huntington said of the right forearm strain that forced Grilli to leave the game Monday night against the Washington Nationals and land on the 15-day disabled list.

There was another reason the players felt good about themselves. They like their chances of continuing their march toward the franchise's first playoff spot in 21 years even if they have to do it without Grilli — the best bullpen hammer in baseball this season — for a couple of weeks or more.

"We're lucky to have Mark," first baseman Garrett Jones said.

That would be Melancon.

"He's been in that role before," Jones said. "He's got a closer's mentality. He is a closer."

Melancon pitched like one in the Pirates' 5-1 win Tuesday night against the Nationals even if he didn't get a save. He needed just seven pitches to take down Anthony Rendon, Ryan Zimmerman and Adam LaRoche in a one-two-three ninth inning.

Pirates manager Clint Hurdle said he went to Melancon in a non-save situation for a couple of reasons. The Pirates will face the Nationals' two best starters — Stephen Strasburg and Gio Gonzalez — in the next two games and might not have a late-inning lead to protect. The ball also travels well in Nationals Park — "A four-run lead is like a three-run lead here," Hurdle said — especially when it's hot.

"Who sets that [three-run save] line, anyway?" Hurdle asked. "They had the middle part of their order up. Let's put our best on it and see if we can move on."

Melancon and the Pirates did just that.

Melancon's experience as a closer should not be underestimated. He converted 20 of 25 save opportunities for the 2011 Houston Astros. Yes, that was a bad Houston team, and Melancon is pitching for a pennant contender now. But he knows the pressure that goes with the job. He knows how difficult it can be getting the final three outs of a game. He knows blowing a save after his team works three hours to build a lead can make for a hurtful loss.

"I did it in college [at Arizona]. I did it in the minor leagues. I did it in Houston," Melancon said. "I had more

Mark Melancon came on in the ninth inning to close out the Pirates' 1-0 win over the Cubs on May 22, 2013.

experience doing it coming into this season than Grilli had."

The Pirates aren't wrong for thinking Melancon will be just as successful.

"Look at what he's done in the eighth inning," Huntington said. "He not only doesn't give up any runs. He doesn't allow any baserunners."

That wasn't much of an exaggeration. Melancon's 0.95 earned run average is best among National League relievers. He has been scored upon just four times in his past 40 games.

"I hate the word perfect," Pirates second baseman Neil Walker said. "But he's been damn near perfect."

That's why everyone on the Pirates was surprised when Melancon pitched into big trouble Sunday against the Cincinnati Reds by walking two hitters. Trying to protect a 3-1 lead, he had to face All-Star Joey Votto with the bases loaded and no outs.

"Votto in that situation? That's not a comfortable feeling," Huntington said.

Melancon got Votto to hit into a 3-6-1 double play, getting over quickly to get the second out at first base. He then got All-Star Brandon Phillips to bounce out to shortstop. Grilli came on in the ninth to get his 30th save in 31 chances in a 3-2 win.

"Mark is a lot like Jason was for us last season," Huntington said. "He's not afraid to face the heart of the lineup in the eighth inning."

Or the ninth inning, for that matter.

"I take the ninth inning the same way I do the eighth," Melancon said. "What could I do differently, anyway? My approach stays the same."

Walker put it into words.

"Pound the strike zone ... Strike one! ... Strike two! ..."

"It's all about attacking," Melancon said.

"He does the same thing every time. He goes right after the hitter," Walker said. "He knows what he's doing is working. So why change? He never tries to take it to a different level. That discipline is so important, especially for a late-inning guy."

It helped Melancon make it to his first All-Star Game last week, a difficult achievement for a set-up man. He's a big reason the Pirates bullpen has the second-best ERA (2.76) in baseball. The team is 45-2 in games when it led after seven innings.

Now, someone will have to fill Melancon's eighth-inning role. Hurdle said he will use a committee, deciding his man or men each game based on matchups and his gut feeling. Tony Watson, Bryan Morris, Justin Wilson and Vin Mazzaro each figure to take a turn. Morris pitched the eighth Tuesday night, giving up just a single.

"I feel like any of us in the bullpen can step up and get big outs," Melancon said. "I wouldn't necessarily say what we've done is amazing. It's a lot of hard work and a lot of talent plus some uncommon camaraderie. Some things have gone our way, but things tend to go your way when you work hard and have talent."

Melancon played for the 2009 world champion New York Yankees. He's not afraid to say these Pirates have similar potential.

"I know what a good team looks like. I know how it acts and how it feels. This is a standout group. We've got good people. Not just good baseball players, but good people. I really enjoy my teammates. There aren't many egos in here. It's a really good group that has a chance to do something really special."

Melancon's teammates share his positive vibes. They seem convinced he will keep the team on track until Grilli gets back, hopefully sooner rather than later.

"Mark doesn't have to change anything," Jones said. "He just has to be Melancon."

That should be plenty good enough. ∎

Mark Melancon closed out the ninth in the Pirates' 10-7 win over the Reds in April, their first series sweep of the 2013 season.

NOTHING BUT THE BEST

Pirates Sweep Doubleheader, Own No. 1 Record in Majors and 1½-Game Lead

By Michael Sanserino · July 31, 2013

A rookie pitcher, a fiery veteran, a couple outfield bloopers and Alex Presley's wild, walk-off single in the 11th inning of the opener lifted the Pirates to a doubleheader sweep of the St. Louis Cardinals Tuesday that also gave them the best record in baseball.

The Pirates beat the Cardinals in the first game, 2-1, and 6-0 in the second, turning a half-game deficit in the National League Central race into a 1½-game lead in the span of a few hours.

They also moved to a season-high 22 games over .500.

"This is a great baseball town," manager Clint Hurdle said.

"This was a great baseball town for a long time. We're making every effort to make it a great baseball town again. … We've covered some distance, but we've got more to cover."

In this highly anticipated five-game set against the Cardinals (62-43), the Pirates (64-42) already have assured themselves a series victory by winning the first three games.

Rookie pitcher Brandon Cumpton pitched seven shutout innings against the best offense in the league as the Pirates won the second game.

Cumpton struck out five, walked one and allowed three hits to earn his first major league victory in a spot start. He was recalled from Class AAA Indianapolis earlier Tuesday to help the Pirates pitch through two games in one day.

"I just tried to fill it up, throw strikes, and my defense made plays," Cumpton said.

It was the best start of Cumpton's career, which spans four outings, all spot starts. He started the year 13th on the team's starting pitching depth chart, but Tuesday he led the Pirates to one of their biggest wins this season.

"I thought his overall command was the best we've seen since he's been up," Hurdle said. "All his pitches came into play."

Cardinals outfielder Matt Holliday misplayed two balls in left, including a fifth-inning, two-run homer that bounced off the heel of his glove and into the left-field bleachers. It was the 15th home run for Andrew McCutchen, and it gave the Pirates a 4-0 lead.

In the next inning, Holliday slammed into the wall about three feet away from where Josh Harrison's ball connected with the padding as Harrison raced to a leadoff triple.

From then on, Holliday was heckled by many of the 33,861 in attendance, especially those in the left-field bleachers who, apparently, took advantage of 17 uninterrupted innings of beer sales.

"We love the support," Hurdle said. "They've been great. We want more.

"We've probably got to do more to earn more from them. Everybody's got their own level of confidence for when they're going to buy in. And there's probably still some waiting to see."

In the first game, Presley provided the win.

After fighting his way to a full count, he hit a ball up the middle that looked like a double-play opportunity for the Cardinals.

But reliever Kevin Siegrist tried to snag the ball out of the air and instead deflected it away from second, allowing Russell Martin to score and the Pirates to celebrate.

"It's a good thing he tipped it," Presley said.

"I don't know if he would have doubled me up or not, but to get a hit right there was awesome."

A.J. Burnett allowed one earned run and three hits in seven innings, striking out nine and walking three in his sharpest outing since he returned from the disabled list earlier this month after a strained right quad. ■

Alex Presley is congratulated by teammates after hitting a game-winning single in the 11th inning against the Cardinals in the first game of a July 30, 2013, doubleheader.

A.J. Burnett and Russell Martin celebrate the Pirates' complete-game win over the Rockies on August 4. Burnett's previous complete game was on July 31, 2012, against the Cubs.

PUSH TO THE PLAYOFFS

BLOWOUT LOSS DOESN'T RUIN A GREAT WEEK OF BASEBALL

Cardinals Turn Over NL Central Lead to Pirates

By Gene Collier · August 2, 2013

For most of the past month, this rare five-game entanglement between the Pirates and the St. Louis Cardinals loomed on the calendar like an ominous and perhaps even fateful crossroads, yet when it finally came around, both teams rolled into it with little evident apprehension.

The Pirates and Cardinals knew the one thing about this series that maybe we didn't care to know because it might have taken the fun out of it, that it would only turn out to be really significant if somebody swept it.

Despite the gathering of another massive North Shore crowd, this one carrying dollar store brooms and frothing to see St. Louis get skunked in a five-game series for the first time in 97 years (seriously, 1916), the Redbirds put a big fat purple 13-0 bruise on Clint Hurdle's pitchers Thursday night and got out of town with their dignity.

With their dignity, yes, but without their 1½-game lead in the National League Central Division, which they turned over to the Pirates by losing four out of five.

Had the Pirates swept it and wound up ahead by 3½, or had the Cardinals done the same and pushed the Pirates 6½ games behind, then you might have had something both teams would point to in October as the place where so many things started to go right/wrong. As it is, in terms of relevant Central Division politics, this series will enjoy the approximate shelf life of a hard-boiled egg rolling down the aisle of a PAT bus.

Or something.

It's not like the Pirates haven't been in first place before, and it's not like the Cardinals are about to plunge into a dark depression at the prospect of being 1½ games out with 55 to play.

But as theater, it was little else than the very best essence of the sport.

Baseball must ultimately be adjudicated, obviously, with pennants won, a World Series staged, a champion crowned and another city's heart ceremoniously broken on national television. But it says here that none of that is necessarily better than this, than these past five games, when nearly 130,000 people came out on four perfect summer nights in Pittsburgh and watched the best teams in baseball perform with purpose and passion.

The whole edge-of-your-seat, heart-palpitating-on-every-pitch brand of big-league ball can wait until October as the promised product of what dreams may come, but the game lives for the summer. This was a series that could not have been placed more perfectly than at the intersection of July and August. It was a series to savor, to relax, sit back, talk ball, have a dog or two and a brew or three, and to lament

A.J Burnett allowed three hits and one run in seven innings, with nine strikeouts, in the first game of the Pirates' doubleheader against the Cardinals on July 30, 2013.

nothing except that PNC Park could be here for another 50 years and never produce a more perfect showcase.

In practical terms, the Pirates proved they could beat the very best competition in a variety of ways, shutting 'em out (6-0), outlasting 'em in 11 (2-1), spanking 'em hard (9-2), coming from behind (5-4), and proved beyond any doubt they are far from a perfect machine.

Oh yeah, 13-0.

In practical terms, Charlie Morton, the starter Thursday night, worked six shaggy innings to extend a funk in which he has now allowed 38 hits in 30⅔ innings with an ERA of 4.98. He's no Brandon Cumpton.

The Cardinals, always glad to see Morton, lashed him for 10 hits in five innings. St. Louis is 8-2 all time against Morton. Against the Cardinals, his career ERA has swollen to 6.30.

If the Pirates have a part of their rotation squealing with dysfunction, the Cardinals are possibly solidifying theirs thanks to Joe Kelly, 25, who kept the Pirates hitless into the fifth and worked six shutout innings. Starting for only the fifth time in 2013, Kelly has allowed just one run in his past 17⅔ innings.

No one figured him for the stopper when it came to the Cardinals' seven-game losing streak, their first of longer than three all season.

Nine games remain between these teams, six of them in St. Louis, the final one Sept. 8.

Should you be looking for the next fateful scheduling crossroads, the next ominous zombiescape dystopia, you might look past Sept. 8 to the season's horizon, because after that final Pirates meeting, the Cardinals might very well play the final 19 games of the season against teams with losing records.

Nineteen days of Brewers, Mariners, Rockies, Cubs, Nationals and, yes, more Brewers.

A lot will happen between here and there, and perhaps beyond, and maybe it will be more dramatic and more momentous and even more historic.

But it won't be better baseball than the baseball that filled this week.

Can't be. ■

Starling Marte slides home safely for the Pirates in a 5-4 win over the Cardinals on July 31, 2013. The Pirates won the first four games in the five-game series.

ANOTHER ACE UP THE SLEEVE

Burnett Follows Liriano's Gem with His Own, Going Wire-to-Wire to Beat Colorado

By Bill Brink · August 5, 2013

As A.J. Burnett walked off the field in the seventh inning, the cheers began to pick up.

After a 1-2-3 eighth, they got louder, and louder still when he took the mound for the ninth.

The sellout crowd of 37,980 Sunday afternoon at PNC Park realized what was happening. A.J. Burnett was in the midst of an A.J. Burnett start.

"It's been a great season all around, packing this place in," Burnett said. "They know what's at stake. They know what kind of team we have. They know it's different."

Burnett had good command of his knuckle-curve. He struck out batters. He kept batted balls on the ground. He did all those things efficiently enough to pitch a complete game against the Colorado Rockies, giving the Pirates a 5-1 win and ensuring they took two out of three games in the series.

Burnett (5-7) held the Rockies to one run on eight hits. He struck out nine and walked one. The complete game also ensured two full days of rest for the bullpen, including the team's off day today.

"You take pride in finishing what you started. All those guys down there, they could use a break," Burnett said, nodding toward the relievers at the other end of the clubhouse.

Burnett pitched seven innings in each of his previous two outings, but threw 107 and 113 pitches. He needed only 110 to go the distance Sunday, and 83 were strikes.

"He had good command of both the sinker and the four-seamer, and he was just working on the edges," said catcher Russell Martin, who hit a three-run home run in the fifth. "And when he wasn't working on the edges, it was down in the zone and moving. He kept his pitch count low.

"That's one of the things with A.J. He's got such good stuff, it takes him a while to get hitters to put the ball in play and [Sunday] he was just electric."

Burnett received support from an offense that waited out Rockies starter Juan Nicasio and took advantage of the bullpen. The Pirates had eight hits, including three for extra bases. Andrew McCutchen went 2 for 3.

Duress in every inning but one inflated Nicasio's pitch count, and he needed 103 to get through 4⅓ innings. Nicasio (6-6) was charged with four runs on six hits and three walks.

Garrett Jones' game at the plate — 0 for 0 with two walks and an RBI on a sacrifice fly — embodied what the Pirates tried to do against Nicasio.

"He was trying to hit his spots, keep the ball down and away," Jones said. "I think that's why his pitch count was so high, he couldn't hit that spot regularly and consistently. When he made a mistake, we were able to drive the ball. If not, we were taking our walks."

The Pirates had a lead three batters into the first. Starling Marte led off with a double and scored on McCutchen's single.

Despite exiting the game in the sixth inning, A.J. Burnett set the tone for the Pirates' late rally over the Tigers in May to win 5-3. The win marked the first time the Pirates had won 18 games in a month since September 1992.

Neil Walker doubled to start the third and stayed alive to score because of a smart play on the bases. McCutchen singled, putting runners on the corners, and Pedro Alvarez walked to load the bases.

Martin grounded to third. DJ LeMahieu stepped on third, retiring McCutchen and removing the force at home for Walker. LeMahieu threw home, but Walker retreated to third. He arrived there to find McCutchen, who was already out, standing on the bag, momentarily confusing catcher Yorvit Torrealba and preventing him from catching Walker in a rundown.

Jones hit a sacrifice fly, and Walker scored to give the Pirates a 2-0 lead.

McCutchen walked with one out in the fifth and Alvarez singled, chasing Nicasio from the game. His replacement, Manny Corpas, hung a slider on his first pitch to Martin that became a three-run home run.

The Rockies finally scored in the seventh. Michael Cuddyer singled and took second on Burnett's wild pitch. Jonathan Herrera's single scored Cuddyer.

The Pirates improved to 67-44 with 51 games remaining. They are off today before facing the Miami Marlins for three games at home.

"It's a team thing. It's the new Pirates," Martin said. "The 20 years are about to be over." ∎

Above: A.J. Burnett acknowledges the crowd after a complete-game win over the Rockies on August 4 at PNC Park. Opposite: Wearing a special military tribute uniform, Burnett delivers a pitch against the Astros on May 18.

FINDING A HOME

Martin Endures Long Road to Become Catcher, Feels Comfortable in New City

Everett Cook · August 6, 2013

Russell Martin's professional catching career began with a man named Jumbo and almost ended on a slider to the groin.

It was 2002 in the Los Angeles Dodgers' instructional fall league. Martin was a man without a major league position, seen as not quick enough for shortstop, not powerful enough for third base. Off of a tip from Martin's college coach, the Dodgers decided to try him out at catcher.

The first bullpen session went about as perfectly as Martin could have imagined. He was catching a man named Jumbo Diaz, who was well over 300 pounds and threw close to triple digits without much command. For 20 minutes in a squat, Martin caught almost everything with a resounding pop from his mitt. He felt good. The Dodgers felt good.

Next up was Mike Keirstead, who threw in the mid-90s with movement. On the fifth pitch, Keirstead gave Martin a sign he didn't understand. A slider was coming in his way, unbeknownst to the new catcher.

The pitch came in fast and hard, clipping the Montreal native's thumb and hitting him in a spot not ideal for a man to be hit by a baseball. For 20 seconds, writhing on the ground, Martin said to himself, "I'm done. I'm never catching ever again. I'm retiring right now."

He laughs about it now, mainly because the switch worked out. Eight years into an All-Star career, moving to catcher might have been the best thing to happen to this first-year Pirates player.

It was a long, tough journey, one that started with a baby, a tennis ball, and a dad with the perfect work schedule.

JOHN COLTRANE

Russell Martin Sr. and his brothers were watching TV while his 1½-year-old son, Russell Martin Jr., sat on the floor in front of him. A tennis ball the brothers were playing with got away and began bouncing in front of the baby. Bounce … bounce …

Before the ball hit the floor a third time, the infant grabbed it out of the air.

After that, it was just a matter of honing that natural hand-eye coordination. Martin had a bat in his hands at 2 and spent much of his childhood on the baseball diamond with his dad, whose life and schedule worked perfectly for the tutelage.

Martin Sr. is a sax player, and a good one. He would wake up early and go to the Montreal subways, playing for crowds of people on their way to work before hurrying back to go to the field with his son. Almost 20 years later, Martin still remembers the point values of the games that the two used to play. Five points for hitting the ball, three points for hitting the tee.

After working on the diamond, Martin Sr. would go back to the subways for people returning home from work. He played the saxophone during rush hours, with baseball in between, devoting his free time to his child with the middle name of his hero, John Coltrane. The saxophone is a hard

Russell Martin makes play on ball bunted by Cole Hamels for an out against the Phillies on July 4.

instrument to master, but as Martin says, "it comes from the soul."

In third and fourth grade, Martin moved from Montreal to live in Paris with his mom and step-dad, which had some unintended side effects.

"I gained about 20 pounds from eating pastries and stuff every morning stopping at the corner bakery," Martin said, laughing. "I'd crush two to three croissants in the morning and then on the way back home I'd crush one or two more. My dad was so heated when he saw me in the summer."

There was no baseball in Paris, no games with his dad. His beacon became the summer and those lessons with his dad turned coach.

"I definitely missed him a whole bunch but I knew that once summer came I was going to go back and play baseball and hang out with my dad," he said. "If I had baseball taken away from me completely for two years, I would have been miserable. Just knowing that baseball was right around the corner helped me get through it."

WEATHERING STORMS

After graduating from Polyvalente Edouard-Montpetit — an athletics-based high school in Montreal — Martin wanted to attend a two-year university in the United States. He didn't know much about the American school system, so his main requirement was that it was somewhere warm so he could play baseball year-round.

Along with two other Canadian teammates, Martin discovered Chipola College in Marianna, Fla., one of the best junior college programs in the nation.

He played six positions as the super-utility man, including 12 games at catcher toward the end of his final year in Florida. Before the Dodgers drafted Martin in the 17th round of the 2002 draft, Jeff Johnson, his college coach, told Los Angeles scouts that Martin's only path to the major leagues might be at catcher.

Turns out, he was right.

"I just felt like, with his skill set, his competitiveness and his great hands, his gamesmanship and all that, he had a chance to be one of those guys," Johnson said. "Would I tell you that he would be in the big leagues a couple years after I said that? No. I didn't think that would happen."

That doesn't mean the transition was seamless. Martin estimates it took him 2½ years to truly feel comfortable with the new position, having to work heavily with Dodgers coaches to learn one of the toughest positions in baseball at one of its highest levels. Jon Debus, who was the Dodgers catching coordinator and now works in the New York Mets organization, said the two had to "weather some storms together" while learning arguably the most important position in baseball. If a catcher has a bad day, a lot of people have a bad day. The transition was frustrating at times, but according to Debus, the smartest thing they did was stick with him even when Martin's catching future looked bleak. Not every catching prospect gets that patience.

Martin spent four years in the minors before making the jump to Los Angeles in 2006. He finished in the top 10 of the National League Rookie of the Year voting that year, less than two years after he began to feel fully comfortable in a squat.

"You don't want a guy that isn't going to do his homework and work for his pitching staff and be respected — that's so hard to teach, you've got to have that," Debus said. "If you don't have that, you aren't going to be catching for very long. That's an important piece of the puzzle. All the good teams have that guy. The Pirates now have that guy."

AT HOME IN PITTSBURGH

Pirates starter Jeff Locke had lasted just four innings July 31 at PNC Park while giving up four runs and 10 hits against Central Division rival St. Louis Cardinals, but the Pirates had chipped away and tied the score in the fifth inning. The new pitcher was Tony Watson, who gave up a single in the seventh inning. The next batter reached on an error. Tie score, runners on first and second, one out. Martin went to the mound, talked things through and calmed down his pitcher, then retreated back to a squat.

Watson got a groundout and then ended the inning on a strikeout, preserving the tie. In the eighth with a runner on second, Martin took a pitch low in the zone and shot it back through the center of the infield, just out of the reach of the shortstop. His RBI single scored the go-ahead run and was the difference in a 5-4 win.

In 2012, Pirates catchers threw out 19 baserunners. They were the worst in the major leagues in stolen-base percentage and had the lowest non-pitching batting average on the team. By all statistical measures, they were awful.

In the offseason, the Pirates signed Martin away from the Yankees on a two-year, $17 million deal. Signing a player away from New York isn't cheap — Martin makes up about 11 percent of the Pirates payroll this year and was the biggest free-agent signing in franchise history.

And yet, Martin leads the majors in batters caught stealing

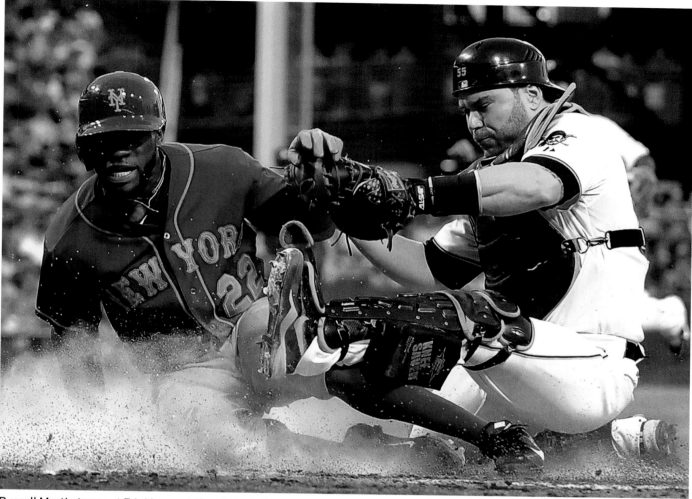

Russell Martin tags out Eric Young at the plate during a July 13 game against the Mets.

with 25. He's sixth in the majors in stolen-base percentage and in the top 10 on the team in batting average, hitting .251 with a .356 on-base percentage.

The Pirates finished 13th in baseball in ERA in 2012 — they are first this year. Not all of that should be credited to Martin, but his presence and knack for pitch framing certainly has helped calm a pitching staff that has weathered transition, injuries and youth.

Martin has been catching for more than 10 years now but still views shortstop as his natural position. That's what he played growing up in Montreal and what he wanted to play for Team Canada in the World Baseball Classic earlier this year before team officials and the Pirates squashed the idea.

"If I put on a different jersey and took off my mask and went out there right now, I would look like a shortstop if people didn't know who I was," Martin said. "People think that because I play catcher I can't play shortstop, but I don't consider myself a typical catcher."

The signing of the atypical catcher made a lot of sense for the Pirates and for Martin. Los Angeles was too laid back, New York was too frantic, but Pittsburgh is like home, Montreal.

In a city with a blue-collar reputation, Martin is fitting right in.

"I love Pittsburgh," Martin said. "The people are down to earth, hard-working. It reminds me of Montreal. This reminds me more of where I come from, as far as the working class. They grind it out." ■

IT'S JUST THAT KIND OF YEAR

Walk-Off Homer by Josh Harrison Clinches Pirates' 4-3 Victory over Marlins

By Gene Collier · August 7, 2013

The third inning Tuesday night brought the annual Pedro Alvarez triple, appearing as it reliably does once every summer around here; you know, like the Steve Miller Band concert.

Big ol' jet airliner, rounding second as the 2-1 pitch he rifled into right-center field settled at the base of the wall. As El Toro achieved the largely unprecedented speeds of an active runway, it couldn't help but occur to you that the roaring PNC Park crowd was probably going to be too loud for anyone to hear Alvarez's hamstring twang like a snapped banjo string.

But it's not that kind of year around here, is it?

No, no, the kind of year it is around here is the kind where Josh Harrison comes off the bench to get the bottom of the ninth started precisely because left-handed reliever Mike Dunn is still in the game after striking out Alvarez in the eighth, and instead of getting it started, he gets it finished by taking Dunn to the seats in right.

The kind of year it is around here is that Alvarez slides joyously in that third inning, belly-first toward the outfield side of the bag, nose-first toward the third-base bag on a night he couldn't seem to find it with his foot or with his better fielding judgment, such as it is.

If you thought Pedro was setting personal speed records toward third Tuesday night, you should have seen him escaping the locker room.

Bang.

Gone in 60 seconds.

Whatever, bro.

That triple tied the score, 3-3, after Andrew McCutchen jump-started the Pirates with a two-run double off Miami's Henderson Alvarez, who shut them out only two weekends ago.

But it was a Pedro error in the seventh, his only charged error of at least three misplays around the bag, that reloaded the bases after McCutchen appeared to bail the Pirates out of that inning with still another galloping-driving-stretching-glove-flashing catch inches above the center-field lawn.

The bases loaded with Fish, .190-hitting Jeff Mathis sliced a 2-1 pitch from Vin Mazzaro that was scheduled for touchdown near the foul line, at which point it seemed only a question of whether Miami would suddenly be ahead by two or three.

But again, it's not that kind of year around here, is it?

No, no, Mathis' shot landed foul and two pitches later he lifted one harmlessly to Starling Marte in left, and some 27,907 settled in to await a more favorable verdict, even if Pedro would again attempt to postpone it in the eighth.

Pirates pitcher A.J. Burnett (right) hits catcher Russell Martin with a shaving cream pie after Martin's walk-off single in the 10th inning gave the Pirates a 5-4 victory against the Miami Marlins on August 8.

Batting with the bases loaded and no one out against a drawn-in infield, Alvarez didn't have to do much more than put the ball in play against Dunn, who lurked in the bullpen nearly three hours for precisely this moment. Dunn fell behind Alvarez, 2-0, then dismissed him on three pitches, the third of which he failed to swing at even though he stared at it real, real hard.

Alvarez is now hitting .213 against left-handed pitching, which has allowed only three of his 27 home runs. Yet the oft-detested lefty-righty thing taketh and it giveth as well, witness the Harrison pie-in-the-face heroics.

When you see that on the same night Mathis' potential three-run triple falls foul, the same night McCutchen saves the game still again, the same night Alvarez rounds second like Omar Moreno and lands in a beauteous pile of baseball dirt, you'd be pressed not to conclude that this is a summer unlike any seen around here in a long, long time.

"Yeah, those are the little things that happen that make you go, 'Yeah, something's going on,' " manager Clint Hurdle said afterward. "We're gonna commit to keep showing up and be a little bit better every time out, but those things, when they do show up, they're feel-goods.

"The more feel-goods ya get, the more you feel good. There's no doubt about it. The more you see things like that, the more confidence it bodes. When [Mathis'] ball turns at the end, three inches foul, to see Pedro go head-first into third, that gets everybody excited. To see Mazzaro come in and, with two pitches, finish that [sixth] inning, all those little things add up."

Things will add up a little faster, of course, when Alvarez stops looking for his first August home run and lifts his average since the All-Star break well past the .197 figure he lugged into the game Tuesday night.

There doesn't seem to be any hurry though, as all of baseball just watches the Pirates proceed at their own pace, skittish as it might be, toward a fast-clarifying inevitability. ∎

Andrew McCutchen slides safely into home plate against the Diamondbacks on August 18.

TURNING FROWNS UPSIDE DOWN

Optimistic Manager Hurdle Leads Pirates to New Heights

By Jenn Menendez

It's been 35 years since Clint Hurdle's smiling mug beamed off the front of a March 1978 *Sports Illustrated* cover, face lit in sunlight, hair parted down the middle, that thousand-watt smile framed by a square jaw.

The story portrayed Hurdle as a phenom in the making — a tale that never exactly played out.

But buried deep among the paragraphs is a description of the Dodge van he tooled around in at age 20: it was fitted with a fold-out bed, refrigerator, spittoon, and a harmonica on the padded dashboard. You can almost hear Lynyrd Skynard crowing from the tape deck.

A lifetime later, on the verge of what could be a very special season in Pittsburgh, it is clear there's a little bit of that kid left somewhere inside the Pirates seasoned manager.

"Oh yes, absolutely," said Hurdle. "There's still a guy who wants to play the harmonica. Never learned. Dabbled on one for a long time. Still like classic rock. Still play classic rock. I'm past the customized van stage. It was as close to a hippie VW bus as I could get."

Hurdle, now 56, is at once a born motivator who instinctually sees the bright side, and an occasional ball of fury, tossed four times this season for arguing with an umpire.

That dichotomy — of an intense and deeply driven man, yet naturally light-hearted and happy-go-lucky — is constantly evident.

When one of his top pitchers struggled in his first start at altitude in Denver, Hurdle found him in the dugout, wrapped two arms around him in a bear hug, wearing a wide smile and a cheek full of bubble gum.

When his 11-year-old daughter called in agony after a series of losses in August, he whipped out a story of Pirates ships lacking rearview mirrors, twisted around a Dr. Seuss metaphor, and turned her frown upside down.

"Clint is very a happy go lucky guy. He never looks at a glass as half empty. He always looks at it as half full," said his father Clint Hurdle Sr. "When he was playing ball in Little League and he'd come home, be upset form a bad game I'd always point out good things along with the bad things. It's where I think it has come from. He can be very serious but he's got a lot of that joking, playful guy in him."

Hurdle was hired by the Pirates in 2010 — long after his playing career ended and after a seven year stint as manager for Colorado — his first major league managing gig.

The Pirates were 18 years into what would become a streak of 20-straight losing seasons.

A former top prospect as a player, Clint Hurdle — shaking Andrew McCutchen's hand during an April 12 game against the Reds — has helped turn around the Pirates during his three seasons as Pittsburgh manager.

In his introductory press conference, Hurdle likened turning the franchise around to how he would eat an elephant: One bite at a time.

"He definitely has his own style. He's like a mix between having a parent, that typical coach, and just like a buddy you'd go have a couple beers with and hang out," said catcher Russell Martin. "He makes it work."

The first two seasons did not end as planned, but the building blocks were there.

Shortstop Clint Barmes, who played for Hurdle in Colorado, said his boss still has that intelligent baseball mind — but made one important distinction: "He's given the players the clubhouse."

"I want them to know I've got their back. I always try to revisit the emotions, the feelings, the facts that came my way as a player and honor those from this office," said Hurdle. "I try and earn their trust. If they don't trust you, you'll never be able to coach 'em up. And that takes time. So they know you care about them outside of being a switch hitting second baseman, a fourth outfielder, your fourth starter, your closer."

This season Hurdle's mantra has been steadfast since spring training: Meet the demands of the game.

Good or bad, it's only one game of 162.

Lose? Shower off and go home.

By July 1 the Pirates were in first place with the best record in baseball.

By Sept. 1, they were locked in a tie atop the National League Central Division with rival St. Louis.

"The one thing that he is, he's consistent with how he treats people. There's no real favoritism," said Martin. "You can still talk to him about whatever you want. You don't feel like you're going to be judged by him. He wants the best for you and he cares about each individual on the team and that's important to me."

On Sept. 2 the team reached 80 wins with another fine start by Charlie Morton.

No. 82 — the numerical mark of a winning season — was on its way.

"This has been one of the most enjoyable seasons I've had in baseball," said Hurdle. "Watching this clubhouse take on its own identity, where the players know they own it. They own the dugout. They own the bullpen. And actually watch them take ownership of things now? The leadership. I've seen the leadership growth in some of our own guys. Then externally, Burnett, like Grilli, like Martin, like Barmes. Their roots have networked off throughout the clubhouse.

"I love the way they continue to play the game regardless of the last three or next three. It's a bunch of boys playing out playing in the backyard. They've been good at that all year."

As for that 20-year string of futility by the franchise?

Hurdle doesn't own it, nor does he let his players.

"We honor the angst and the frustration our fan base has on a lot of different levels," said Hurdle. "But some guys have been here a week. Some guys have been here two years. I've only been here three years. The one misconnection a lot of people have is we haven't been here for 20 years.

"We haven't finished the way we've wanted to the last two years but we've improved the caliber of play and now we've put ourselves in a position to do more and take a bigger step forward. We are committed to doing some big things. We believe we're capable of doing it." ■

Manager Clint Hurdle argues with umpire Eric Cooper after pitcher A.J. Burnett was charged with a wild pitch during the Pirates' 2-1 loss to the Cardinals on July 30.

LIRIANO PULLS IN A JUICY REBOUND

Alvarez, Jones Hit Early Homers to Back Superb Complete Game

By Michael Sanserino • August 15, 2013

Francisco Liriano was looking for a mulligan. Starling Marte was looking for redemption.

Both got what they were looking for Wednesday night, and the Pirates got what they desperately needed — a win.

Liriano pitched his second complete game this season and Marte delivered a two-run double as the Pirates beat the St. Louis Cardinals, 5-1, at Busch Stadium, bouncing back from a disappointing, 14-inning loss a night earlier.

The Pirates (71-48) snapped a four-game losing skid and extended their National League Central Division lead over the Cardinals (68-51) to three games.

The Cincinnati Reds (68-52) are a half-game behind St. Louis.

Five days after his ugliest outing this season, and perhaps his career, Liriano delivered his best start this year, allowing one earned run and four hits to pick up his 13th victory, tying him for the NL lead in wins.

"That was masterful," Pirates manager Clint Hurdle said.

"From start to finish. Talk about pitch efficiency. The first-pitch strikes were there. Punchouts were there. Swing and miss. Sixteen hitters retired on three pitches or less. Just outstanding."

Liriano allowed career highs in runs (10) and hits (12) Friday against the Colorado Rockies. But, if he continues to pitch the way he did Wednesday night, that rough start might be just a blip on an otherwise impressive season.

Liriano used pinpoint control of his fastball to prevent St. Louis batters from getting solid contact on any pitches.

After getting a handful of ground balls in the first couple of innings, he got batters to chase. He struck out six and four whiffed at his slider.

"It was sharp," Liriano said of the slider. "It went where I wanted to."

Catcher Tony Sanchez said Liriano pitched inside early to capitalize on the Cardinals' weaknesses. And, as the game progressed, Liriano went to his strength — a devastating off-speed pitch.

"Started in the zone and ended up out of zone," Sanchez said.

"There was a good foot-and-a-half, 2 feet of movement on that slider when it was good, and it forced a lot of swings and misses."

Liriano saved a taxed bullpen after six pitchers were used Tuesday night.

"Nasty pitches," said Marte, who himself was looking for a do-over after dropping a routine fly ball Tuesday night, turning a sure win into an eventual loss.

Hurdle said Marte arrived at the ballpark Wednesday "in a good place," and he credited the veterans for lifting Marte's spirits.

He said he looked down in the dugout Tuesday night as players were talking to Marte after the fateful error.

"I just made him laugh," Andrew McCutchen said. "Sometimes, that's all you've got to do."

Marte said he was feeling low Tuesday night, and those consolations helped.

"Everybody tried to help me," Marte said.

"I was feeling pretty bad, and they just told me to keep my [head] up."

Wednesday, he was ready to atone for that transgression.

The Pirates already had a three-run lead with two outs in the fourth when Marte stepped to the plate. He cranked

116

Francisco Lirano delivers a pitch against the Oakland Athletics on July 10.

a low-flying liner that just cleared diving shortstop Pete Kozma, scoring runners from second and third to make it 5-0. The ball didn't go into the gap, but Marte didn't care.

He sprinted out of the batter's box and never slowed down until he slid into second, although most players would have been content with a two-run single. He beat the throw from center fielder Jon Jay for his 24th double this season.

Earlier in the inning, Sanchez got his second career RBI to add to an early Pirates lead.

St. Louis rookie starter Shelby Miller was the loser after getting roughed up in six innings. Miller allowed five earned runs and eight hits, walked two and struck out five. Miller has lost his three career starts against the Pirates.

Pedro Alvarez led off the second with a mammoth home run that landed halfway up the grass slope batter's eye in straight-away center

Alvarez crushed a 95 mph fastball from Miller, sending it 440 feet from home plate for his 29th home run of the season, tying him with the Arizona Diamondbacks' Paul Goldschmidt for the NL lead.

Two batters later, Garrett Jones punished another 95 mph Miller fastball with a hooking home run over the right-field wall.

It was the 11th home run this season for Jones and his first since a solo shot July 21 at Cincinnati. ■

A SEASON OF BOUNCE-BACKS FOR LIRIANO

Pitcher Looks to Tie Career-High 14 Wins

By Jenn Menendez · August 19, 2013

In the beautiful marriage of Francisco Liriano and the Pirates, it's unclear exactly who needed the other more.

Liriano's once-electric career was spiraling away. The Minnesota Twins had sent him to the bullpen, then traded him to the Chicago White Sox. His strikeouts were down. His walks were up. His ERA soared.

As winter arrived in December, the Pirates were coming off two late-season collapses.

Liriano needed a fresh start. The Pirates needed a left-handed starter to bolster the rotation.

What transpired has wildly exceeded expectations as Liriano takes the mound tonight one win shy of tying his career high of 14.

As resurrection tales of a player and his team go, they don't get much better.

"I was expecting to do good things in baseball. Finally I'm doing what I always wanted to do," said Liriano. "Having these games is like a relief for me."

Once upon a time, Liriano was a hotshot prospect from the Dominican Republic with a dazzling slider and mid-90s fastball.

He was an All-Star his rookie year in 2006, winning 12 games and amassing 144 strikeouts before he needed Tommy John surgery.

He missed 2007 but returned to win just 11 games in 2008 and 2009 combined. The magic returned in 2010 when he set career highs in wins — 14 — and strikeouts with 201. He was named the American League Comeback Player of the Year.

But between 2011 and 2012 with Minnesota and Chicago, Liriano won just 12 games in 35 starts and had an ERA sailing north to 5.34.

"I struggled so bad the last two years, it was kind of frustrating for me," Liriano said. "I never stopped working and just thank God for a second chance and having this year I'm having right now."

The Pirates sought a left-hander and agreed to terms with Liriano four days before Christmas.

A freak injury to his forearm delayed the process, but he was a Pirate by late January and began the process of rehabbing.

"At first I thought I wasn't going to sign here. I got hurt the night before I was supposed to get my physical done," Liriano said. "They called me and told me they wanted to get a deal done. I was so happy to be here. Happy for the chance to pitch."

Pitching coach Ray Searage and the training staff got to work to get Liriano back to form.

It took just two starts at the start of the season for Searage to see the first glimmer of what kind of year might be in store.

"He's throwing sliders, backdoor sliders for strikes. Then he's throwing changeups for first pitch, then he'll come back and throw a 94 mile-an-hour sinker on you," Searage said. "I'm like, 'This is going to be special. This is good.'"

Liriano's take is simple.

With his fastball command back, he has the freedom to use his slider and changeup when necessary.

After struggling in 2011 and 2012, pitcher Francisco Liriano has returned to the form he showed while making the All-Star team during his rookie year with the Minnesota Twins in 2006.

"Now I can use it any count. Before, I used to probably throw more changeups, sliders than fastball," Liriano said. "Now I just use any pitch — fastball, slider, change — at any point in the count. That made a difference.

"I think it's command. Pitching is all about location. Having a better location with my fastball makes everything better."

Searage said he and the organization quickly took note of his response to that freedom of sorts.

"Because that's Frankie. If I try to make Frankie pitch like Jeff Locke, we wouldn't have what we got," Searage said. "That's force-feeding him to do something that he's not comfortable doing. Frankie does pitch the way he pitches. So just let him be him. That's what we did."

Catcher Russell Martin walked into the batter's box to face Liriano many times in his American League career.

"I don't remember doing anything good. He had a good fast-ball. I'd go up there trying to hit the fastball and next thing you know, I'm hitting a weak ground ball somewhere off a changeup or a slider," Martin said.

Martin suspects the switch to the National League has helped his teammate, but that his good health coupled with a good defensive team behind him are also factors.

"For the most part, he's been super-aggressive getting early strikes," said Martin. "He has the ability to have three plus-pitches. Whatever you choose, any pitch is going to be a tough pitch to hit. He doesn't make many mistakes in the zone and he gets a lot of swings and misses because his stuff is so sharp and hitters have a hard time picking it up. He's been making good pitches."

Last week in St. Louis might have been his best start yet.

He was clobbered in the thin air of Coors Field in Colorado in his previous start — his mulligan, as the team calls it — but recovered to throw a complete game, including eight shutout innings in a 5-1 win Wednesday.

He entered the ninth inning with just 83 pitches, struck out six, walked one and never looked fatigued.

"That was masterful. From start to finish," manager Clint Hurdle said. "He's embraced this opportunity and this team. It was an opportunity for him to be a stopper and he went out and took care of it."

Heading into tonight, Liriano has 13 wins and a 2.68 ERA with 45 walks and 113 strikeouts.

It has been a long time coming.

"I don't know, everything was different this offseason," Liriano said. "Everything happens for a reason. You never know." ■

In his first year pitching in the National League, Francisco Liriano has anchored the Pirates' starting rotation.

MORTON SETS THE BAR HIGH

Recovering from Surgery, Starter Just Keeps Getting Better

By Bill Brink · September 3, 2013

Charlie Morton wants to change the context of his starts. He does not want to measure his performance against the backdrop of his recovery from Tommy John surgery. He wants to judge himself in the closest thing to a vacuum as possible.

"I'd like to base where I am off of what I did last start," Morton said.

If Morton keeps pitching the way he has, his previous start will keep the bar high. Morton performed well again Monday afternoon in a 5-2 win against the Milwaukee Brewers at Miller Park. The win gave the Pirates 80 in a season for the first time since 1992.

Their next win will guarantee a .500 or above finish for the first time since that season.

The Pirates have won four of their past six games after losing three in a row.

Morton improved to 7-3 after his sixth consecutive good start. He allowed two runs, one earned, and seven hits in seven innings.

He walked two and struck out six.

"Guys have to respect his velocity, guys have to respect his sink," said Neil Walker, who hit a three-run homer. "When he's getting them with two strikes, he's mixing in that breaking ball and that split. He's pretty tough when he's ahead in the count."

Morton worked masterfully with his curveball once he found it later in the game. He struck out the side in the sixth on 10 pitches, using the curveball as the final pitch of each at-bat.

In the seventh, after an error gave the Brewers a run and a man on third, Morton used the curveball to strike out Jonathan Lucroy and end the inning.

"Today was probably the one day he didn't have [the curveball] as a go-to," manager Clint Hurdle said. "It showed up later."

In Morton's past six starts, he has allowed eight earned runs in 41⅓ innings for a 1.74 ERA.

He has allowed two or fewer runs in each.

"He went out there and pitched his behind off," Pedro Alvarez said. "Got guys to make weak contact, and, when we needed a ground ball, he got that ground ball. He's been pretty darn good all year."

Hurdle and Morton noted that Morton's split-change has worked well in recent outings. Morton stopped throwing the pitch when he first returned to the majors in June, he said, but brought it back to provide another off-speed offering if he can't command his curveball that day.

"I feel like my sinker is good enough to get through the lineup a couple times, but then, you know, guys are going to be all over it if you keep throwing one pitch," Morton said.

Tom Gorzelanny allowed a single to Morton, the only batter he faced in the seventh, before shoulder tightness forced him from the game. Jose Tabata got his third single before Walker hit one an estimated 423 feet into the second deck in right. Walker's 10th homer of the season put the Pirates ahead, 5-1.

"I knew the guy threw a lot of fastballs and he threw hard, just wanted to get the foot down and get a barrel on something," Walker said.

After coming back from Tommy John surgery, pitcher Charlie Morton rebounded to post the best season of his six-year career in 2013.

Tabata went 3 for 4 with two RBIs, driving in Clint Barmes each time.

Alvarez squashed a possible Brewers scoring chance in the third.

Norichika Aoki singled to right, then took second when Marlon Byrd bobbled the ball. A groundout sent Aoki to third, and the infielders moved in. Lucroy grounded to third, and Alvarez threw home, catching Aoki in a rundown. After retiring Aoki, Alvarez wheeled and threw to second in time to nab Lucroy, who attempted to advance, and end the inning. Alvarez has an arm strong enough to make the play, and it took a perfect strike to do it.

"You never want a guy in scoring position," Alvarez said. "We were just fortunate that we were able to tag Aoki quick enough to be able to get a play at second." ∎

NO REASON NOT TO THINK 'WIN IT ALL'

Pirates Acquire Morneau, Buck and Bird in Late-August Deals

By Ron Cook • September 1, 2013

The St. Louis Cardinals aren't going to roll over and give the Pirates the National League Central Division title just because the Pirates added a quality left-handed bat in Justin Morneau Saturday, a mere four days after the Pirates acquired Marlon Byrd and John Buck. Nor are the Cincinnati Reds, for that matter. But that doesn't change the wonderful truth this morning. The Pirates are good enough now to take the division. They are good enough to win it all. The division. The National League pennant. The World Series.

Everything.

"We do [believe that]," general manager Neal Huntington said late Saturday afternoon. "People probably will mock that statement, but we do."

Huntington and the Pirates get no ridicule here. They are absolutely right to feel good about their team and its postseason chances. They have as much chance to win as any of the other National League clubs that will make the playoffs — the Cardinals, Reds, Atlanta Braves and Los Angeles Dodgers.

Let's look at what the Pirates are bringing into September beyond their 79-56 record and one-game lead over the Cardinals in the division race after they spanked the Cardinals again, 7-1, Saturday night at PNC Park:

- Three quality starting pitchers in Francisco Liriano, A.J. Burnett and Charlie Morton. Burnett was strong Saturday night, holding the Cardinals to one run and four hits in seven innings.
- A bullpen that has been baseball's best all season. It will get even stronger when Jason Grilli returns, perhaps this week.
- A lineup that picked up 17 home runs and 74 RBIs with Morneau, who was acquired in a trade with the Minnesota Twins. That's on top of the 21 home runs and 71 RBIs from Byrd and the 15 home runs, 60 RBIs and catching depth from Buck that came in a deal Tuesday with the New York Mets. Byrd made a difference in his first game with the Pirates with a three-run home run in a win against Milwaukee. Morneau, who is hot after hitting nine home runs in August, is expected to start today against the Cardinals.

"Justin is excited," manager Clint Hurdle said.

No kidding.

Not long after the trade was announced, Morneau jumped on a plane in Dallas-Fort Worth, where the Twins were playing, made it to PNC Park in the fourth inning and was in uniform on the bench in the sixth. He couldn't wait to take his first crack at the Clemente Wall in right field, although he wasn't needed Saturday night. That eagerness to get to a new team is a pretty good measure of a man's excitement.

"We're all excited," Hurdle said.

Why not?

Huntington has put the Pirates in an excellent spot. The pitching and defense have been strong all season, but the offense frequently was lacking even before Starling Marte went on the disabled list. Now, with Morneau and

Acquired from the New York Mets along with Marlon Byrd, veteran catcher John Buck provides the Pirates with catching depth as they chase the franchise's first postseason berth since 1992.

Byrd, "The lineup plays out longer," Hurdle said. Russell Martin can bat seventh — where he belongs despite hitting a home run Saturday for the second consecutive game — instead of fifth. Garrett Jones and Gaby Sanchez no longer have to get so many at-bats at first base because of Morneau. There no longer is a bottomless hole in right field with Byrd. Jones can get some starts in right with Byrd moving to left if Jose Tabata falters. A healthy Marte will provide another huge boost when he returns to left field, perhaps by mid-September.

"To add two guys like that, we're very fortunate," Hurdle said of Byrd and Morneau. "We're a better team. We're a stronger team. We have a lot more options than we did four days ago."

Give some credit to Pirates ownership. Bob Nutting agreed to take on about $2.5 million in salary in the Morneau trade. That's real money.

"I think it's just more tangible evidence of what we've been doing," Hurdle said. "They backed up their talk and words with action."

Give more credit to Huntington. Hurdle praised his "persistence" in getting Morneau, Byrd and Buck. Huntington was able to add three quality major leaguers in exchange for three minor leaguers and another player still to be identified or cash.

All along, the Pirates could win games with pitching, defense and, occasionally, speed. Now, they can win more often with a three-run home run from someone other than Pedro Alvarez. Did I mention Byrd hit one Wednesday night? He went 2 for 4 Saturday with a double, an RBI and a run scored.

"It makes Clint's job a little easier because he has more weapons," Huntington said. "It gives him a lot of options. He can pick the match-ups based on the pitcher …

"We're a deeper, more talented team. Our defensive versatility is better and we've upgraded our bench."

There are no guarantees, of course. There never are in sports. The Penguins thought they did what it took to win the Stanley Cup last season when they added Jarome Iginla, Brenden Morrow, Douglas Murray and Jussi Jokinen before the trade deadline. A lot of us believed that. But the team came up well short.

Sure, the Pirates might not do better in October than one wild-card game on the road.

But Huntington believes the club is built to go a lot deeper. So does Hurdle. So do the players.

I'm not willing to argue with them. ■

Outfielder Marlon Byrd, who set a new career high in home runs in 2013, homered in his first game with the Pirates on August 28.

Pirates outfielders (from left) Felix Pie, Marlon Byrd and Andrew McCutchen celebrate as they come off the field following the Pirates' 7-1 win over the Brewers on August 28.